BLACK GENIUS

BLACK GENIUS

Essays on an American Legacy

TRE JOHNSON

DUTTON

DUTTON

An imprint of Penguin Random House LLC
1745 Broadway, New York, NY 10019
penguinrandomhouse.com

LIBRARY OF CONGRESS CATALOGING-IN-PUBLICATION DATA

Names: Johnson, Tre author
Title: Black genius : essays on an American legacy / by Tre Johnson.
Other titles: Essays on an American legacy
Description: [New York, New York] : Dutton Books, [2025]
Identifiers: LCCN 2024050547 (print) | LCCN 2024050548 (ebook) |
ISBN 9780593186473 hardcover | ISBN 9780593186497 ebook
Subjects: LCSH: African Americans in popular culture | African Americans—
Social life and customs | African Americans—Social conditions |
United States—Race relations | Johnson, Tre | African Americans—
Philadelphia—Biography | Philadelphia (Pa.)—Biography
Classification: LCC E185.625 .J646 2025 (print) | LCC E185.625 (ebook) |
DDC 920.0092/96073—dc23/eng/20250422
LC record available at https://lccn.loc.gov/2024050547
LC ebook record available at https://lccn.loc.gov/2024050548

Printed in the United States of America
1st Printing

BOOK DESIGN BY LAURA K. CORLESS

The authorized representative in the EU for product safety and compliance is
Penguin Random House Ireland, Morrison Chambers, 32 Nassau Street,
Dublin D02 YH68, Ireland, https://eu-contact.penguin.ie.

For my unwavering Day 1s—
Wanda, Kendra & Sean

CONTENTS

West Philadelphia cowboys, July 2023. Photo courtesy of Tre Johnson.

INTRODUCTION   ix

PART I

CHAPTER 1

   Your Best Bet Is All-Negro Comics!: *Graphic Novels and Black Culture*   3

CHAPTER 2

   Streemal: *Navigating America's Education*   39

CHAPTER 3

Live Right, Do Right, Fight Like Hell: *Family and Legacy* 77

PART II

CHAPTER 4

The 5th Dimension: *Celebration in America's Face* 113

CHAPTER 5

What Doesn't Kill You Only Mutates and Tries Again: *Performance in the Streets* 139

CHAPTER 6

Agitate! Agitate!: *Black Paranoia™ and Surveillance* 173

PART III

CHAPTER 7

The Branch That Came Back: *Communities and Neighborhood Transformation* 205

CHAPTER 8

Vimeo Killed the Internet Star: *Black Folks in the Digital Age* 229

CHAPTER 9

The Imagined World: *The Future Black World* 261

ACKNOWLEDGMENTS 287

INTRODUCTION

Name one genius that ain't crazy!
—Kanye West, "Feedback"

As a person who steps in and out of Black worlds, I am often exposed to how the rest of the world sees us. I watch on social media, in art galleries, at music festivals or on weekend nights downtown, how Black people strut and flutter our various beauties at everyone else, sometimes as a signal to each other, sometimes as an act of defiance to the rest of the world. We're utterly amazing, yet Black folks are consistently, persistently, intentionally, conveniently, diabolically left out of conversations about genius all the time. That is why this book exists. I think America knows this but has repeatedly resisted our genius to the point of mutual destruction.

BLACK GENIUS is a series of knowledgeable observations. I've watched how the world seems to both be infatuated with and infuriated by Black presence; we're seen as a boon and a burden. None of that has stopped a total excavation of our existence—our

creativity, resiliency, majesty and intensity have been on the ca-
daver table for generations now due to the several somethings
that happen within awe-inspiring Black identities and experiences. In *BLACK GENIUS*, I define the concept of "genius" by
looking at the intersections of how we've used our cultures,
identities, histories, communities and values to augment not
only how we talk about and explore ourselves in America's con-
fine, but also how we better the country for everyone. Black genius is about how we leverage what might typically be seen as
disadvantages—our marginalized, "low" placement in society;
our Blackness; our communities—and flip them into a series of
superpowers. It is about how despite the cyclical nature of white
America granting and then retracting political, social and financial liberties to Black Americans when it served them (wars, vot-
ing, housing, employment rights, etc.), we have managed a series
of cultural ingenuities to press forward.

I wrote this book in admiration of our long, continual ability
to reshape culture to do our bidding. It's about how malleable
we've always had to be to evolve our humanity: our joy, our in-
ventiveness, our grief, our pursuits, our history and our movement. These types of genius have looked different in our uses of
language, fashion, music, education and community.

When I think of genius, the graffiti-style airbrush tee comes
to mind. The style was made obsolete in another example of
white America's greed for exploiting Black culture. You know

the airbrush tee, that non-fussy shirt you could find at mall kiosks, Black block festivals and on the corner. The ones sold "on
the side" by someone's cousin or out of the trunk of a car. The
ones hung up on display in urban wear shops and sneaker joints
in the hood.

The airbrush tee was the hood apparel for a certain time in the
'90s. Customized airbrushed tees of literally anybody could
be made by the artist. You could get your girl or boy (or both
of y'all) spray-painted onto a white tee. You could get Aaliyah
(complete with sunrise/sunset dates and shades) on a white tee.
You could get unofficial re-creations of rap album covers or
Black slang. You could be a walking, loving obituary to your relative, best friend, lover, classmate, whoever. The shirts might've
looked cheap and tacky to a lot of people, but the airbrush tee
was all heart, all skill, all DIY. It remains symbolic of how Black
people find inventive ways inside of a racist, capitalist America
to show each other love. These airbrushed tees with their sometimes hard-to-figure-out renderings ("Is that Mary J. Blige or
Janet Jackson?"), bright colors, graffiti-style lettering and itchy
T-shirt material were the kind of thing a lot of people avoided
and mocked.

But fast-forward to the 2020s and you'll see how the airbrush tee became another Black genius casualty in America's

exploitation of Black culture. Nowadays, everyone from big box stores to fashion boutiques to Etsy shops have strip-mined Black mourning and turned it into profit. Of all the types of artifacts that we use to mourn—the hanging sneakers on overhead lines, the teddy bear and flower altars on city corners—these businesses selected the custom tee. You can buy RIP-type tees of Biggie, Aaliyah and Tupac everywhere from Gap to Target, from online shops to boutique stores.

Devoid of the grieving process, these tees are now nostalgia products marketed and manufactured back to everyone as a way of conferring authenticity and coolness. As clothing clout-chasers, they say, "I was into this Black shit before you were." A couple of years ago while vacationing in Northern California, I was shopping in a local downtown when I popped into a women's boutique clothing store. There among the racks of high-end bedazzled jeans, thin-knit cardigans and floppy sun hats, I saw an artificially worn-looking oversized sweatshirt with a crowned Biggie selling for $130.

The Biggie sweatshirt was made "vintage"-style by a line called Daydreamer. The product description for the sweatshirt reads:

> With his lyrics often telling the tale of his own life—hardship and criminality, debauchery and celebration—we leave you with an authentic portrait of the renowned rapper paying tribute to

his last photoshoot just three days before his death. Accented in gold glitter and designed on a French terry raglan crew that's fitted, yet breathable.

Biggie's on a French terry raglan crew for $130 now, his death a literal selling point. A far cry from the $10–$20 airbrush tee. Now it seems like it was all a dream. Daydreamer's Biggie sweatshirt is a great mini example of the weird relationship between capitalism and Black culture, especially hip-hop. It's a story of how so much of Black DIY culture gets gobbled up and repackaged, and how it can lose its meaning and authenticity once it becomes mass-produced. There's something incredibly chilling about seeing this through Biggie's arc: a brother who once freestyled outside of NYC bodegas and street corners, rose to mainstream fame, and was shot and killed, and was then reconstituted as so much product that his story, his life, his meaty-mouthed delivery and sweaty swagger are now all fodder used to sell expensive sweatshirts aged to look like the wearer has been a hip-hop Day One'er, that they've endured the same battles to hold on to culture, to this man and his music, longer than you.

The airbrush tee culture saw a mix of dying down and leveling up after the '90s. It was sometimes a nostalgic flex signaling a type of authenticity and realness to the street as culture's cyclical nature brought a series of '90s aesthetics back. Drake, for example, famously wore an airbrushed Aaliyah tee several years ago, while other rappers like YG and Kanye revived the style in conjunction with album releases and Yeezy promotions. At its heart is customization, and customization is uniqueness, and uniqueness is individuality, and individuality requires some measure of independence and creativity—that's why the airbrush tee owes its origin to '70s and '80s graffiti when Edwin "Phade" Sacasa got started with the idea back in NYC.

But like many things we create, airbrush tees started being co-opted by bigger brands and companies, especially places like Disney and Warner Bros., keen on how urban artists were using characters like Bugs, Mickey, Elmer Fudd and Donald Duck in Black-read, urban styles and affects. They took the concept and mass-produced it, and that eventually led to what we see now: scores of fast-fashion tees at Target or online at ASOS repackaging decades-old album covers, pop stars, songs and cartoons. This has pushed the airbrush tee back into the margins of the hood, while Alexander Wang repurposed the idea in the 2010s during New York Fashion Week. The airbrush tee is the perfect example of the culture that's been taken out of our hands and reproduced for mass consumption, and which has required the work of cultural archivists to keep its Black, hip-hop roots alive. It's also a microcosm of how something we do may first be ignored, deemed ghetto, or criminalized—either literally or culturally—before it becomes accepted and appreciated for what it is.

I wrote *BLACK GENIUS* to applaud the amazing things that we do every day at every level. I initially set out to write about schools and schooling people, about performing and showing out, about drawing and "you drawn." I wanted to show and remind us that we're incredibly special and that the world's often incredibly lucky (and rich!) because of what we bring to the table in a country that's often made us cut the tree, build the table, serve the table, haul the table—but rarely allowed us to sit at the table.

That's what I've been thinking about in coming to *BLACK GENIUS*, and it's truly been about coming to it versus it coming to me: These are stories about what's always been there, how we always do, highlighting what's "been been." We been doing creative things. We been in society's lab, mixing and creating things. These are the ways that we survive, find joy, express love, push out anger, cycle curiosity, elevate beauty—through genius.

Our genius has been contested by politicians, institutions, authorities, cultural gatekeepers and sometimes our own people. It has been scrutinized along lines of classism, sexism, colorism, queerness and whiteness. Black writers, thinkers, children, entertainers—white-collar, blue-collar, gay, straight, single, partnered—have often worked twice as hard to make the case for ingenuity, articulation, mobilization and humanity in our daily existence. Our blood and bones have so thoroughly soaked into the ground here, and yet America still resists the notion that we can lay claim to any kind of greatness, whether that be in what we do for ourselves or for the country. Currently, we're watching forces reappropriate the intention and goals of DEI, roll back policies like affirmative action, disinvest from Black creative content and journalism and stymie access to entrepreneurship to grow our own businesses and wealth.

During the pandemic, when everything was shut down and lots of Black and brown people in particular were scurrying around the city on bikes to deliver takeout, groceries and cravings, I walked Christian Street in Philly's Graduate Hospital neighborhood on St. Patty's Day. There, I saw hordes of white people flagrantly violating the grouping and distancing rules. They were covered head to toe in green hats and tees, or had their faces painted with splotches of leprechaun green as they passed under apartment and row-home windows blaring Black music.

In January 2020 I wrote an essay for *Slate* called "Heard but Not Seen" about how tense it feels being at restaurants, coffee shops and gym classes where the music is often Black but the clientele isn't. I shared an experience at Toups South, a now-closed New Orleans restaurant located in the Lower Garden District. While I sat there eating a fried chicken sandwich, A Tribe Called Quest, Jay-Z, Kendrick Lamar and a track from *Lemonade* came on at different points on their curated playlist. The sensation of being in a mostly white restaurant playing this music in post-Katrina NOLA made everything from the restaurant to the patrons to the cultural context feel disconnected: "patrons occasionally singing along with little snatches of lyrics, the bartenders' heads bopping as they mix drinks, the chefs in the center island chopping to the beat." It all brought up the issues around appropriation, cultural extraction, gentrification and the sort of dark-humor irony of how often our music is good enough but we aren't.

I know somebody out there is like, "Is this really genius, though?"

My grandparents were born in the 1930s, and when I think about the backdrop of what they lived through and directly or indirectly survived—hangings, burnings, displacements, hard-shell racism, everyday use of the word "nigger," callous segregation and discrimination—and how they still found ways to fall in love, build a family, buy a home, get cars, take trips to Atlantic City, spoil grandchildren—Yes, I think to myself, Yes, this is something that I want to write about. Yes, I think to myself, I do think this takes some measure of genius.

My mother's father, Robert Lee Murphy—"Pop-Pop"—had a patriarchal presence in our family. We'd talk about football (we were in Trenton, and while we had the choice of several regional NFL teams, Pop-Pop chose the Eagles, so therefore we were all

Eagles fans) and Michael Jackson, who Pop-Pop was both marveled by but also found to be "weird" in that way that made it clear that I should never be that kind of weird. Similarly, he loved Prince—or rather, he gave Prince some grace with his weirdness because Prince was often surrounded by gorgeous women. He hated that Prince had his little butt out, but he also hummed along to "Kiss" every time it came on. He also loved Beyoncé, who he called "Bouncy." Robert was a man of consistent taste.

I don't think my Black people are any more unique, smart, savvy or brave than other Black people located anywhere within the north, south, east and west borders of the United States. I don't think my Black people are of a time or circumstance that made our journey as a family more privileged or singular. I don't think we started any further along the bases than any or every other Black folks during that time. My Black people did what I know a lot of Black people—maybe your Black people if you're Black and holding this book—did: We took stock of what this country and what white people would and wouldn't give us and we found a way. We continually, relentlessly, inventively found a way.

No, my goal is to either confirm or convince or remind you that genius has permeated every porous corner of Black American subculture out of both ingenuity and necessity. This isn't a single-story mythology of Black people making use of America's

scraps, a narrative that food historian Michael W. Twitty so elo-
quently clapped back at in a tweet once: "PLEASE STOP SAYING
SOUL FOOD CAME FROM WHITE PEOPLE'S SCRAPS. It's a
complete lie that robs us of our agency, ownership, creativity
and resistance and shows a lack of critical thinking and cultural
literacy." His words might be a summation of this book, which
is an intentional, much longer clapback at the idea that Black
people just make do. There is authentic, original genius within
the Black community—in ways that don't make everyone comfortable (quite the opposite, actually), don't always serve the
Great Engine of the American Dream, don't always present
themselves as fodder to be reconstituted by white and non-Black
people (though Lord bless them for always trying)—and this
genius isn't tied to the notions of the scraps that white people
have left us. Our genius exists both within and despite the
American experience and is unquestionably ours.

I find it fascinating how often I've had to debate this notion
of Black genius with people. For many people, "genius" has become the cerebral version of "beautiful," so heavily applied that
it loses meaning because we've become overly generous with
our notions of how or where it exists. If I'm being honest (I'll be
honest with you in this book, honestly), there's also an unspoken skepticism among some people who hear me and an earnest
desire among others to talk about Black genius because it might
feel like part of the rightsizing and reckonings that have crested

and fallen over the last several years in particular. In place of the ever-elusive financial and emotional acknowledgment of reparations, some of the cultural movements and conversations we have around Black humanity can feel, to a cynic, like lip service: Leaders, friends, acquaintances, institutions, governments, maybe even lovers can often, in the immediacy of seeing some type of viral Black harm or death, offer the assurance that they will commit to supporting us more, hearing us better, improving themselves and "shaking up the status quo." At this point, it makes sense why a lot of us have stopped holding our breath when we see or hear these gestures: America rushes in and recedes around supporting our humanity when and as it serves its own interests.

You'll perhaps see some of the same waxing and waning inside this book. You'll see the simple truths of what many of us witness or implicitly know and don't speak on, the ways that our steady march forward can rather exasperate collective America's appetite for Black people, and within that, for our genius. It's true, as a result, that a measure of what we do and produce is tethered to the circumstances that America created around us. But the brilliance is in the bravery to transform those circumstances into genius ways of living, creating art, building community or pushing against the boundaries that have been created around us. It's brave because it means we're chancing to make people around us uncomfortable, brave because it means that we might be trying something unprecedented and authentic, brave because there are often social, political and cultural consequences to Black folks being brave. *BLACK GENIUS* broadcasts the many ways Black people have striven to make our art, our voices, our politics and our communities better. And I want to show that our genius has abounded in corners of American culture in ways that we don't typically examine, and make sure, as a result, that we spend some time looking at and considering the corners we don't often look at.

Like, can Black motorbike riding in the streets of Baltimore, Detroit, DC and Philly really be considered "genius"?

What's it mean for Black identities and culture to be co-opted? Is that a sign of our genius?

In the social media sphere, where Black people are endlessly tossing content into the digital void, they're also routinely being lifted and stolen from. Clearly, there must be something that people see about the genius we're creating in those spaces.

For a community of people long surveilled, what does it mean to continually leverage ways to skirt Uncle Sam's eye? That, too, is genius.

And even if they're familiar corners—Black neighborhoods and communities, art museums, cultural festivals, graphic novels, the workplace—hopefully we're all thinking about and considering unfamiliar things that illuminate Black people's genius. Doing so brings a greater appreciation for how the multitudes each of us contain allow us to express ourselves creatively, politically and socially. When we shine light on these examples, we're actually creating ongoing cultural legacies. Elements of every one of these genius types can be part of a larger blueprint for how we continue to both maintain and iterate what makes the Black American experience and perspective so beautiful and powerful.

Talking about genius is strenuous. It just really is. And it's likely you're going to want to challenge and discard some of the examples in this book.

But what you'll grapple with will depend on whether you can accept a broader, cultural definition of genius—particularly when it comes to Black people. We routinely watch society anoint prodigy, once-in-a-generation, "voice of a generation," genius titles to white people throughout time, and yet so infrequently is the title ever applied to Black folks in wider conversations. Is Kanye maybe right then: Does it ironically take Black geniuses being "crazy" to be taken seriously as an above-average intellectual? And what's that even mean?

Of course Kanye isn't right, but Kanye's still a genius (I will defend that in conversation; not interested in doing that in this book), and one purpose is to uncomfortably nudge all of us to think more broadly. There are books that examine Dave Chappelle, Nina Simone, Prince, Yasiin Bey (Mos Def), Lauryn Hill— all these bright, shiny luminaries that are household names. Tiger

Woods, O. J. Simpson—all these comfortable, familiar names of Black people that had reached the zenith of their excellence and then, eventually, cruelly, sometimes temporarily, toppled.

But writing something in that vein would have been a cheat code of a book. That was an easy out that probably wouldn't do much but reconfirm stories and idolatry that we were already familiar with. And some of these people might still make a cameo in this book (we love a good cameo; some of our favorite songs got cameos in them), but it's more important to talk about people a level or twenty below public awareness. I want to look at the forgotten genius that I see among Black people in everyday life and society.

I decided to write this book because I'm infatuated with Black humanity, intelligence and creativity. I am enthralled by our ability to create something out of nothing and something out of something. We've comfortably expanded and entrenched the definitions of Black beauty and Black pride, but there is still some hesitancy to definitively describe Black genius. I decided to write this because we tend to have restrictions on what we think of as Black genius. I wanted to look at genius from every possible angle, mirroring what I've seen around the country. I wanted to develop levels—my community likes to say, "There's levels to this shit"—and challenge you, me and the world to consider how truly imaginative and beautiful and intelligent Black people can be.

BLACK GENIUS

PART I

CHAPTER 1

Your Best Bet Is All-Negro Comics!

Graphic Novels and Black Culture

Debut cover of All-Negro Comics *in 1947.* Photo courtesy of DigitalComicMuseum.com.

*Cause I'm standing here scratching in my pants pocket
And I can't find the key.*
—Louis Jordan, "Open the Door, Richard"

Kendra and I stand in the cold snow stamping our feet like horses, drilling our soles into the earth. My bunched shoulders are two fists on my back. I am cold, but I am beyond excited. It is February 2018, in Paris's second arrondissement, and we're standing in a line that wraps around the theater block—a racial kaleidoscope of people, all of us in winter coats, puffing our breaths and blowing on our hands in the cold alongside Le Grand Rex's wall. Inside the old-school movie theater, brass railings and wide-mouthed staircases lead to balcony seating. I stare at the red pulpy velvet curtains that shroud the screen. It seems as if no one can simmer down; everyone is buzzing about, laughing and jittering, tossing around energy like real-world vibranium. Truthfully, I'm not sure we can sit down; I don't even really remember sitting down.

By the time the curtains pulled back, Black folks of every hue up in the balcony with us were already clapping, already happy, already chanting:

"Black Pan-ther! Black Pan-ther!"

That night, the theater brimmed with enough energy to

power Paris. Every once in a while I'd glance around and see the occasional non-Black person looking around with a mixture of confusion and awe. Maybe they understood being excited, but they didn't get this.

The theater was ours. The entire room felt like Wakanda, our own fabricated escape from everything that waited outside. Even with all its corporate complications, *Black Panther* was still the type of moment that a lot of us had been waiting a lifetime to see.

I'd just turned forty years old, but staring at that screen as the movie started, the roomful of people shook so hard that the tears balancing at the edges of my eyes fell out. Bewildered with enthusiasm, I simultaneously sat in the present and the past. The young version of me who grew up on comic books would've never dreamt of that moment, even though for years he tried to make his own world, too.

My cousin Sean and I were two teenage comic book–loving Black boys in the '90s whose imaginations could only conjure white superheroes. At least they felt white. Sean's creation was a spandex-clad masked vigilante named Mister X who wore on his full-masked face a top hat that he could toss like Oddjob in *Goldfinger*. Me? I'd created a nameless hero who had Wolverine's upturned hair embedded with remote technology that allowed him to be controlled. He had pupilless eyes (couldn't draw eyes), armored shoulder pads (why not?), a belt braided with pouches and armed gauntlets around his wrists. In my best drawing of this hero, he stood with one knee propped up on a lab table, one arm jutting across his body at a diagonal. In the background, his creator, a white male scientist, looked up at his invention with a mixture of hope and fear as his hand rested on a lever that would bring the creature to life.

On Saturdays, we'd go to the local comic-book store, Steve's Comic Relief, and then we'd sit in Sean's basement with McDonald's takeout. After reading our latest haul of comic books, we'd get sketchbooks and No. 2 pencils, and doodle heroes and stories that sprang from our heads.

Our favorite superheroes at the time were Spider-Man, Batman, Captain America, Silver Surfer and the X-Men, so of course our brains were stuffed with the cotton-white idea that those heroes were far superior to anyone else. And while Black superheroes also existed at the time—Captain Marvel, Black Panther, Storm, Luke Cage, Static Shock, Black Lightning and others—they were considered second-rate heroes, not always treated seriously or placed front and center like the ones who "mattered." They might've looked like us, but we weren't looking at them for inspiration the same way we did the white ones, who were the stuff of lunch boxes, video games, T-shirts, posters and Halloween costumes. When we jumped off beds and climbed trees, we weren't Black Panther or Goliath—we were Spider-Man, Wolverine and Batman.

Me and my cousin Sean playing Nintendo. Photo courtesy of the Johnson family archive.

We didn't know that while we were reading these comics, a secret war was happening against Black superheroes and creators. But eventually it became clear to me that when Black people get to write and create stories in the graphic novel and comic book format, everything from the storytelling to the politics and social commentary gets worked into superhero lore in ways that separate these stories and creators from the pack. And what Sean and I didn't know is that when we'd stepped into the comics world, there was already a long, sometimes broken history of Black heroes on and off the page. Still, every time they were given a chance to really shine, Black creators working on Black characters produced undeniably powerful stories with the ability to punch up.

The first couple of panels on the page quickly set the scene. It's early morning at Pop's Bar-B-Que when two Black men in dark suits walk in. One walks over to the jukebox and starts to select a song. The other stands before Pop's lunch counter. Neither addresses him immediately, but before they do, they agree that they'll knock down the brother in the white apron behind the counter and then smash the place for as much money as possible. But, before getting down to business, the brother at the jukebox in the corner picks a song, and after a moment, Louis Jordan's voice can be heard plaintively singing "Open the Door, Richard" over the tinny, yellow machine's speakers. In just a few moments more, the two brothers—sweet-suited in colorful overcoats, their eyes shielded behind sunglasses, collars popped—menacingly move back towards the restaurant's namesake, and in a flash they wrap his neck in a chain, choking him unconscious.

Black comic book history started with 1947's *All-Negro Comics* created by Orrin C. Evans, a Black man who was raised by Black middle-class parents in Pennsylvania. After dropping out in the eighth grade, Evans became a journalist covering racial segregation stories. He was sometimes referred to as "the dean of Black reporters" for his work at *The Philadelphia Record*, where he was one of the only Black journalists writing for a mainstream white publication at the time, as well as at the Black-owned *Philadelphia Tribune*. At the height of his career in the 1940s, he reported on the duality that Black soldiers faced: fighting for the country on the wartime front lines but returning to face violent racism. Orrin C. Evans believed race relations were gradually going to get better in America.

But his journalism career was making him doubtful. Not enough journalistic coverage stories centered or reflected Black American life, so in 1947 Evans created *All-Negro Comics #1*, a comic anthology of Black stories that Evans hoped would reach Black audiences more than the white stories, heroes and adventures that were the medium's sole focus. *All-Negro Comics* contains eight different Black genre stories—everything from detective tales to jungle adventures. He worked with an all-Black team, bringing together former *Philadelphia Record* colleagues like Bill Driscoll and Harry T. Saylor as writers, and also recruited Black pencilers and colorists. Evans's vision for *All-Negro Comics* was to create something that possessed "high moral and educational standards."

It's this vision that makes him a genius; he recognized early on that a medium like comic books could be a vessel for carrying messages to Black people at a time when very little pop culture spoke to us with any sort of dignity or imagination. On the opening editorial page of the comic, Evans states that *All-Negro Comics* is "another milestone in the splendid history of Negro journalism" that will "give Negro artists an opportunity gainfully to use their talents, but it will glorify Negro historical achievements." *All-Negro Comics* was published a mere six years before *Amos 'n' Andy* finally ended and almost a decade before *Gone with the Wind* appeared in theaters. Depictions of Black Americans still lagged behind those of white Americans. *All-Negro Comics* was Evans's attempt to start pushing back.

The first story in *All-Negro Comics*, "Ace Harlem," is billed as an ode to "the outstanding contributions of thousands of fearless, intelligent Negro police officers engaged in a constant fight against crime throughout the United States." It features a Black Dick Tracy analogue who fights crime in the hood. "Ace" opens with "Open the Door, Richard" playing from a local bar's jukebox as two Black hoodlums come in and shake down the Black owner, and then follows them before eventually introducing Ace, who's on the case to track them down and put an end to their potential crime spree.

All-Negro wasn't just a series of hard-boiled detective tales, though. "Dew Dillies" is an adventure in nature that follows Bubbles and Bibber, two young pixie-like Black children. "Dillies" lets them frolic irreverently and innocently in this setting, as an antidote to the mainstream, mean-spirited impish "pickaninny" depictions of Black children. Bubbles and Bibber get into innocuous, inconsequential trouble like eating a clam and musing about cooking a nearby sitting duck they spot in a pond.

Instead of being portrayed as buzzing worker bees or lazy ingrates, the characters are fantastical: Bibber has wings and Bubbles the lower body of a mermaid. Bubbles and Bibber are wide-eyed, in contrast to the impish drawings that white people used. Bubbles and Bibber aren't stealing farmers' animals and crops or from kitchen tables. They aren't grinning, watermelon-devouring sprites or roving with a pack of wild-haired "savages." They're happy, and "Dillies" is about the happiness and imagination that all Black children should have.

Perhaps the most curious chapter of *All-Negro*, though, is "Lion Man," the story of an "American-born, college educated . . . young scientist" who is dispatched by the United Nations to the "Magic Mountain" on the African Gold Coast. Lion Man is an international watchman whose mission is to prevent any foreign poachers from stealing the large deposits of uranium located there. In this story the poachers are two white men: the mad scientist Dr. Sangro and his jungle navigator named Brosser, who are shown skulking in the African jungle, making their way to a potential uranium deposit.

Lion Man isn't alone, though. He's got a sidekick named Bubba, a stereotypical African native written to be mischievous and accident-prone, who speaks in broken English. Lion Man possesses keen senses and superior strength, and together, Bubba and Lion Man are ultimately able to thwart Dr. Sangro and Brosser's attempt to steal the uranium, despite Bubba's constant bumbling.

As an African protector of a precious resource who is vigilant against interlopers, *All-Negro*'s Lion Man bears striking similarities to a more well-known Black African superhero, despite predating him by almost twenty years. Unfortunately, Lion Man and the rest of *All-Negro Comics*' characters would never appear again; not long after its debut, many of the comic's sponsors and distributors would disappear, and Evans would step back from trying to get another issue out.

Part of *All-Negro*'s challenge was that during the same period, bigger, established publishers began creating Black-themed comic book content. Fawcett Comics and *Parents* magazine released their own Black titles, including *Negro Romance* and comic book bios on Black athletes like Jackie Robinson and Joe Lewis. As several comic book historians have pointed out, Evans and *All-Negro* were fighting an uphill battle—while they didn't dominate the market on Black content, they were the only player in the market that was all Black in distribution, creation and content. Evans's vision was the right call, but it's likely that *All-Negro* had too many supervillains to beat at once: Racial, cultural, financial and political industry power dynamics were too formidable. For all their page power, neither Lion Man nor Ace could topple the real-world forces stacked against them. It would be almost twenty years before America would get its first proper Black superhero when Black Panther was created in 1966 by Stan Lee and Jack Kirby.

It obviously didn't stop with Black Panther. The '70s and '80s saw a sort of Black superhero boom; we started appearing in *Uncanny X-Men*, *Superman*, *Justice League of America*, *Captain America* and *Teen Titans* in attempts to boost sales, appeal to more readers and better reflect the times. You probably know a lot of these characters by now thanks to their popularity and adoption into movies and cartoons, but it's also wild to think that many—Luke Cage, Storm and Bishop of the X-Men, Captain America's partner the Falcon and Black Lightning—were all created by white or non-Black creators.

Evans probably would've been happy with a lot of these Black characters; many of them came from the sort of dignified backgrounds and occupations that I suspect he wanted to showcase in the long term through *All-Negro*. Characters like Sam Wilson (*Captain America*'s the Falcon), James Rhodes (*Iron Man*'s War Machine) and John Stewart (Green Lantern) were former military men. Jefferson Pierce (Black Lightning) was an urban high school principal, while Vic Stone (*Teen Titans*' Cyborg) was a straight-A student and star football player. These guys were cape-on, cape-off heroes with admirable, clear, straight-line morals and attitudes that made them appear more palatable to the largely white male audience comic book publishers were catering to.

You felt that, too. Comics were already a geek habit in most people's eyes, and specifically a white boy one at that. When I started reading them in the '80s because my dad would have heaps of weekly comic book issues sitting on his coffee table with the mail, I'd scoop them up and read them in my bedroom or the back of his car but never quite felt comfortable telling or showing other kids around me that I was into them. I started wanting to draw superhero characters in part because my middle school classmate Max would sit in social studies class sketching them on notebook paper or in drawing pads. I mimicked both his style and his choices—heroic and stoic Captain America, Silver Surfer, Colossus and Spider-Man—which meant I was immersed in the world of white superheroes and didn't even consider drawing any of the Black ones. Add to this bedsheets, cartoons and Halloween costumes, and it became hard, especially as an already-geeky, bookish Black kid in mostly white classes, to show up and show out as a comic book fan.

Evans would've been overjoyed to know Dwayne McDuffie and Christopher Priest, two Black comic-writing geniuses who managed to turn the industry and some of its biggest characters inside out. I loved reading these guys when I was growing up even though I wasn't paying attention to who was writing comics at the time. But I remember some of their biggest moves in comics. McDuffie's *Damage Control* wasn't the kind of comic I'd normally read—it was a satirical comic book series about heroes like Captain America, Spider-Man, Iron Man, the Avengers and other Marvel heroes having to deal with a company responsible for cleaning up the messes they created fighting villains in NYC. You'd pick up an issue of *Damage Control* and find yourself reading scenes where Captain America has to talk billing prices with a construction foreman, or where She-Hulk found herself in the middle of breaking up union fights.

I read McDuffie's darker shit, too, though; he reimagined the *Deathlok* series in 1990. Previously, *Deathlok* had been about a white guy whose body was partially composed of machinery who was sent out on missions to kill and destroy. But when McDuffie took it over, he made the main character Michael Collins, a Black Philadelphia computer programmer whose employer, Roxxon, removes his brain from his body and places it into a Deathlok body, and Collins has to fight the killer programming and corporate control that his former bosses have over his body. I remember finding that comic angry, and scary; in his Deathlok body Collins's face looks like hamburger meat, and there was always something suffocating about knowing his brain was in a body he could barely control.

I didn't know it then, but McDuffie was pulling on all kinds of sources to write this version of Deathlok. Before starting at Marvel he'd been a sci-fi novel and magazine copy editor, and he appreciated history, especially Black history—one of his *Death-lok* storylines was called "The Souls of Cyber-Folk," a play on Du Bois's text *The Souls of Black Folk*. And when you look at this arc in particular, you see the tics of McDuffie's genius at work— once the series' premise was established in the first issue, in the second issue he immediately moved to bring Collins's Deathlok into the Black Marvel Universe, having him partner with Black female private investigator Misty Knight. Together, they try to save a community of autonomous cyborgs like them—Misty has a cybernetic arm but is otherwise human. In teaming them up, McDuffie was able to speak to Black readers as well as white readers about the cultural complexities and experiences of Black Americans. In their first scene together, Misty pitches Deathlok on joining her in investigating why cyborgs are starting to dis-appear, and even though he at first says no, he quickly changes his mind when Misty warns him that he could be next. What's said next between them sounds on the surface like a conversa-tion about cyborgs between cyborgs, but it's really a metaphor standing in for Black people in general.

"Actually," Deathlok says, "I didn't think I was in any danger at all. But the prospect of meeting other cyborgs, of talking to people who have already been through the same things I'm go-ing through now . . . Well, that's just too good an opportunity to pass on." He closes the conversation with, "But if we're going to be spending a lot of time together, you gotta stop calling me

'Deathlok.' My name is Michael." Those are the cool moments you'll get from a specifically Black writer with some cultural awareness and a vision for how to make Black characters work and have meaningful conversations that other creators might not think of. It's not that Black characters haven't or didn't interact with each other in comics before moments like this; it's more that in the hands of a skilled Black writer like McDuffie, you get to watch a genius at work who takes a sci-fi comic book concept, infuses a Black character into it, pulls together other characters to positively reinforce aspects of the character's Blackness, and mixes it all together into a subtle metaphor that doesn't hammer non-Black readers over the head with a message or pander to Black readers as if we don't get what's going on.

Priest is just as good at this with a slightly different flair. While he's also got tons of writing credits to his name, in addition to holding the title of being the first Black staffer to work for Marvel and DC Comics, he's probably best known for his work on *Black Panther*. Priest took on the title character back in 1997 after Black Panther had essentially spent years on the Marvel shelf collecting dust being little- to underused. Priest worked on *Black Panther* for five years, and in that time created several unshakeable legacies for the character. Like McDuffie, he was savvy about cultural dialogue; both McDuffie and Priest saw opportunities to add nuance to the reputations of Marvel's and DC's popular, predominantly white superhero teams, often through their interactions with their Black characters. In a classic exchange between Black Panther and the Avengers, Priest touches on a dynamic that might feel relatable to a lot of us.

The scene features the Black Panther talking with the rest of his Avengers teammates, and during a lull in superhero action, one of them turns to T'Challa.

Firestar: "You said you thought the Avengers might be a threat—so you joined—to investigate them . . . or . . . maybe I misheard you . . ."

Captain America: "Did we all mishear you—?"

Black Panther: "No. You did not."

It's a cool, cold scene that informed much of how future stewards of Black Panther and 2018's *Black Panther* movie came to understand the character. While most characters see joining the Avengers as a badge of honor (and even as readers, you're typically hyped to see your favorite characters get an invite to join), T'Challa accepts membership from a more tactical, aloof position. It's also a move and a characterization that puts a bit of a buffer around Black Panther; by defining his participation on the team by his terms, he's vaulted from being seen as a side character to a strong one. Through that wariness—a mix of allegiance first and foremost to Wakanda as her king, but also a tinge of Black Paranoia about the true intentions of a white superhero team—Priest carved out a cultural space that Black Panther's prior depictions only hinted at.

Scene from Christopher Priest's Black Panther *"Enemy of the State" storyline dated 2002.* Image courtesy of Marvel Comics.

Priest would be responsible for deepening Wakanda's politics and religion by doing far more intentional world-building than writers before him, resulting in additional Priest creations like the female warrior retinue called the Dora Milaje, and government agent Everett K. Ross, a character Priest created as a stand-in for white readers (and editors) to experience Black Panther's world through his fictional eyes and temperament. Ultimately, Priest's five-year run on *Black Panther* was like a Black biblical chain: His run begat Reginald Hudlin's, which ultimately begat Ta-Nehisi Coates's recent historic run as Roxane Gay and Eve Ewing simultaneously wrote Black Panther–world comics, with Ewing eventually taking on the *Black Panther* series herself years later. Thanks to Priest's creative genius, *Black Panther* is enjoying its longest continuous run ever of being penned by Black writers.

Off the page in the real world, both men also waged heroic battles with their comic book peers. Priest was in and out of the comics industry; his frustrations around race, opportunity and creative voice often turned him off writing comics. Priest continued to push comic book boundaries and editors all the same. *Xero*, a 1997 comic about a Black government assassin who disguises himself as a white man, was a Priest-created story cut short by DC Comics after twelve issues. Around the same time, he also created *Quantum and Woody*, a buddy comic about two friends—a white guy and a Black guy—paired up as superheroes, inspired in part by the pairing of Woody Harrelson and Wesley Snipes in *White Men Can't Jump*. Still, it never seemed enough. Priest shared with McDuffie and other Black folks in the industry a similar complaint and observation; for all the work they did busting their asses to write amazing stories for Black characters and the occasional team book, they were never handed the keys to the white flagship titles like *Iron Man*, *Spider-Man*, *X-Men*, *Superman*, *Batman*, somehow never quite ranking high enough in the cultural hierarchy to merit those legendary gigs.

McDuffie famously pointed this out in an internal mock pitch he sent as a memo around the Marvel offices. Called "Teenage Negro Ninja Thrashers," it shaded the company's latest wave of new Black teen skateboard-riding characters by suggesting that they be grouped together to form a new superhero team.

"When a group of teen-aged negroes find cosmic-powered skateboards," wrote McDuffie, "their lives are forever changed!" The premise ultimately wasn't as absurd as the reality that Marvel was really fucking up when it came to these characters, most of whom eventually faded into the background.

Years into his career McDuffie continued to find ways to poke fun at the comics industry—one of my favorite examples being a Justice League storyline where the Black female superheroine Vixen visits an alternate reality that has its own version of the Justice League. Among them is the Brown Bomber, a

Dwayne McDuffie
Proposal for a New Series
"Teenage Negro Ninja Thrashers"
First Draft, 12/13/89

In the past year, 25% of all African-American super-heroes appearing in the Marvel
Universe possessed skateboard-based super powers. In an attempt to remain on the
cutting edge of comics , I hereby propose a new series that will fully exploit this exciting
new trend...

Teenage Negro Ninja
THRASHERS

When a group of teen-aged negroes find cosmic-powered skateboards, their lives
are forever changed! A team of distinct characters join together, swearing an oath to
use their powers for good.

ROCKET RACER: A black guy on a skateboard.

NIGHT THRASHER: A black guy on a skateboard.

DARK WHEELIE: A black guy on a skateboard.

And their leader, the mysterious black guy on a skateboard known only as "that
mysterious black guy on a skateboard."

This is a sure-fire hit as it contains all of these popular elements:

• Circa 1974 clothing and hair-styles

• Bizzarre speech patterns, unrecognisable by any member of any culture on the planet

• A smart white friend to help them out of the trouble they get into

• They're heroes who could be you (if you were black, I mean...)

• They're on Skateboards!

• They have an attractive, white female friend to calm them down when they get too
excited.

Face it Pilgrim, this one's got it all!!!

Have I made my point?

Photo of Dwayne McDuffie's internal Marvel office memo titled "Teenage Negro Ninja Thrashers"—December 1989. Image courtesy of Marvel Comics.

Luke Cage–like Black superhero whose civilian identity is actually a white man that Vixen describes as a "fat guy in street
clothes." In order to transform into the Brown Bomber, he needs

to utter the phrase "Black power!" The scene is actually a nod to DC Comics' own racial history; a character named the Black Bomber was originally pitched to be one of the first Black superheroes in their publishing line. The original idea was similar to a Bruce Banner/Hulk premise; the character's civilian identity would be a racist white man, and he would turn into a Black man whenever he got angry. While the idea was quickly nixed, McDuffie uses this alternate universe as a "what could have been" peek at one of the company's dark secrets, while also sending up the tense real-world dynamic of white creatives working on "cool" Black characters. This has been an active ongoing phenomenon of white creators both creating new Black superheroes and getting to write them—sometimes in the characters' own titles.

I started reading a lot of McDuffie's work a couple years ago after coming across a tweet thread where people were praising his work. In this thread, I not only learned about the "Teenage Negro Ninja Thrashers" memo but also saw the huge love people had for the work he'd done. McDuffie died in 2011; I remember seeing the news pop up on a comic book site that I read to stay on top of industry news, releases and fan takes. At the time, I'd only vaguely known his name; I knew about his work on DC's animated *Justice League* series mainly because I always thought it was so clever that the show not only squeezed in and made the brother John Stewart *THE* Green Lantern on that series, but also that so many of the episodes actually featured John, giving him great social commentary one-liners and a love interest in Hawkgirl, and including him on a lot of the big missions.

Curious, I dove into his work, digging around online and into Marvel's and DC's digital libraries, reading issues sometimes in order, sometimes at random. Reading a lot of those stories, some of which I've mentioned or will mention in this chapter, made me feel like a kid again, discovering comics for the first time through the weekly stacks that sat on my dad's coffee table each weekend I stayed over.

I felt both amazed and embarrassed that I had missed so much of McDuffie's work—the bone-dry wit in his comics, the sleights of hand he used to slide in social topics and political perspectives. His love for and stewardship of comic book characters, especially Black ones, and just how much he got the voices of these characters right. Reading enough of his work—not even all of it, but enough of it—you'd be hard-pressed to think of any reason why this man shouldn't have also done the big, solo household comic titles that featured Superman, Batman and Spider-Man, instead of only getting to weave his ideas into the team books, cartoons, B-level (or C-level) heroes and satirical comics.

Like Brian Azzarello's 2002 *Cage* series created with artist Richard Corben. Released under Marvel's mature line MAX, it involved the already updated Luke Cage, who had swapped his trademark Afro, canary-yellow shirt and chains for a shaved bald head and street clothes, and took him even further.

What's further look like? Like this—

"Who's gonna fuck with me? I'm the scariest nigga ever was!"

Azzarello and Corben's *Cage* series ended up as nothing more than a white person's wet-dream fantasy about the Black ghetto. Corben's illustrations look and feel like comic book pulp smut; Cage's body is beefed up and veiny, his mouth laced with gold fronts, and his street-smart, calm demeanor is replaced with a colder, more apathetic persona. The series dials up all the wrong stereotypes of Black people, drawing heavily from the "modern" Blaxploitation era and understanding of the Black people in the city, setting most scenes in strip clubs and basketball courts, corner stores and ruddy apartments. For a while, it seemed like Luke Cage couldn't catch a break in the comics; the 2016–17 series *Cage!* by *Dexter's Laboratory* creator Genndy Tartakovsky leaned on the most violent and sexual aspects of Blaxploitation and ramped them up to *Ren & Stimpy* cartoonish levels.

White creators continue to use Black comic book characters, and stories continue to cosplay race in ways that often go sideways. The 2010 series *Afrodisiac* by Jim Rugg and Brian Maruca positioned itself as an ode to the '70s, particularly the Blaxploitation era, and in their hands, the series is a pastiche of that decade's loudest tropes. The title character Afrodisiac is a slang-slinging, woman-bedding, kung fu–fighting Black super-bad brother, meant to remind fans of Richard Roundtree, Luke Cage and the assortment of Black male street personalities who defined that time by being violent, cool and always DTF.

Intended to be homages, these types of graphic novels, even when they attempt to be earnest, always end up feeling cartoon-ish and one-dimensional. Entire swaths of these narratives leave out or can't conceive of any sort of real layers or additional context to give these characters depth. It feels like they're simply avatars for these creators to live out immature fantasies.

And even when white creators attempt to tell important racial stories using Black characters, it tends to go awry. In 2017 Boom! Studios published the graphic novel miniseries *Strange Fruit*, by writer Mark Waid and illustrator J.G. Jones. *Strange Fruit*'s premise is essentially, "What if a Black Superman/messianic being landed in the Jim Crow South?" Here, the story's Superman is called the Colossus, who crash-lands from outer space and ends up in the fictional small segregated town of Chatterlee, Mississippi, on the eve of the Great Mississippi River Flood of 1927.

Strange Fruit relishes depicting the racial context of that time. In Chatterlee, Black people are routinely threatened with physical violence, hounded by white locals both hooded and un-hooded and unduly forced to risk their lives by buttressing the town against the fast-rising Mississippi River floodwaters while the white townspeople oversee and watch. All of this is snatched from real historical context that was part of Waid and Jones's motivation to tell this story as two men with a Southern up-bringing.

But everything else about *Strange Fruit* is insultingly bad. The first issue closes with a full-body illustration of the Co-lossus (whose name is revealed to be Johnson), immaculately sculpted, veiny muscled and mute (he will never actually speak in the series), with the Confederate flag wrapped around his lower half. Behind him, a Black farmhand named Sonny stands satisfied as he looks on and remarks, "Awww, yeah. Them white folks really ain't gonna like that." The series spends most of its time setting up the next scene for readers to watch either the Colossus or any of the Black Chatterlee townspeople get vio-lently beaten. In an interview to promote *Strange Fruit*, the two creators talked about being "Southern natives who grew up dur-ing the Civil Rights wars . . . we both feel like we've got some-thing personal to say about the racial clashes we saw and experienced first-hand as boys," and that in itself is supposed to justify this work.

It's hard to think that the issues McDuffie, Priest and other Black creatives faced seemingly went unnoticed as stories and depictions like *Cage*, *Cage!*, *Strange Fruit* and others continued to be not only greenlit but also celebrated. It's also the reason why, forty-five years after *All-Negro Comics*, Priest and McDuffie, along with their Black artist peers Denys Cowan, Michael Davis and Derek Dingle started Milestone Media, the first-ever major Black- and brown-oriented superhero universe (although Priest helped start Milestone, he left before it launched). They created Milestone for many of the same reasons that Evans started *All-Negro Comics*; Black folks on and off the page just weren't getting treated right in mainstream comic books. In the Dakotaverse—the name of the world that Milestone comics took place in—characters like Icon, Static Shock, Hardware and the Blood Syndicate members were Milestone's Black analogue answers to mainstream comics' Superman, Spider-Man, Iron Man and supergroups like the Avengers and Justice League—the constellation of white heroes that these creatives were often locked out of meaningfully working on. Their stories instead lived in an almost exclusively urban context and addressed racial and political politics directly with an explicitness and fervor that no longer had to be fed through a cultural and editorial sluice.

Milestone's timing was culturally significant—the '90s were a tipping point in Black pop culture, with Arsenio Hall, *In Living Color*, Spike Lee's *Malcolm X*, *Def Comedy Jam* and West and East Coast rap's steady rise as an emblem of American identity. The imprint should have latched onto that momentum, and in some ways it did; several of its titles ran for dozens of issues, and Static Shock eventually tipped into the mainstream in both comics and animation. But while Milestone lasted longer than Evans's venture, by 1997 there was virtually no trace of the publisher or its titles.

Still, I know that I struggled to get into Milestone when the comics first came out. I remember the first time I saw *Hardware* sitting on a shelf at a comic-book shop at Woodbridge Center mall in Jersey. My cousin Sean and I always went to comic-book stores at every strip mall and shopping mall we were dragged to, and that one had prominently displayed *Hardware* alongside the row of Marvel and DC titles. I looked at that comic trying to make sense of it—again, you have to remember that even in the early '90s Black superheroes weren't hardly the norm, and it was definitely even less common to see them front and center on their own comic. And they were the niche of a niche hobby; when you were a kid with only a couple of allowance dollars, you were doing early budgeting, you know? Weighing when to take the chance on any new comic was serious business, even when they were characters you knew, so I have to admit that back then, choosing to buy *Hardware* was a leap. Black comic book characters tended to disappear under the cover of night, fading into the background of superhero teams or having their series suddenly canceled. So buying that issue of *Hardware*—which I didn't do that day, but Sean did—felt like it would only end up disappointing me. He wasn't joined by Spider-Man or Wolverine, he wasn't throwing shots at the Hulk or locking Mister

Sinister in a choke hold or deflecting Doctor Doom's beams. No, instead the Denys Cowan-drawn cover featured this new, mysterious Black character in a mech suit, nonchalantly balancing a bulky, blade-edged chain and looking directly out, not even at me but sorta through me, with these black, heavy-lidded eyes. His whole vibe exuded the coolness and the confidence you'd want to launch a new character, a Black one especially.

Hardware's stance gave the air of a rapper or an NBA baller; that cover gave the aura of *Vibe* and *Slam* magazines, which in hindsight proves to me that Cowan and McDuffie knew what they were cooking with, what they were going for. The long chain weapon playfully dangles from the fingers of his left hand like he's holding some drip to show off. The colors were subdued, and the color scheme of Hardware's armor hinted at Afrocentrism—dabbles of black, red, yellow. The whole presentation comfortably pushed pro-Black. It was just him, just you, just the scene, and that was a powerful introduction to a hero, a new publishing line, a new era for comic books. Milestone's other titles had their own distinct flavor—Icon was giving Black Batman-and-Robin vibes, while urban superpowered crew Blood Syndicate was like looking at a hip-hop squad.

But the center of Milestone, for me, starts with Hardware and that iconic cover.

Long live McDuffie, long live Black heroes on and off the page.

But there's traces of Milestone, Priest and McDuffie in to-day's comic book landscape. Together, those stories were influential; they got major comic book publishers to reconsider the opportunities found working with Black creatives and telling Black comic book stories. And so, when the industry eventually reopened the door to Black stories and characters, people leapt through. A lot of this can be traced back to cultural moments like Obama's election and BLM, the former being such a cultural zeitgeist that comic book publishers Marvel, DC, Image and Devil's Due all found ways to take advantage of it. From 2008 to 2012, Obama made comic book appearances in everything from *The Amazing Spider-Man*, *Youngblood* and *Savage Dragon* to *Archie Comics*. In DC Comics' 2009 line-spanning miniseries *Final Crisis*, writer Grant Morrison introduced Calvin Ellis, an else-world version of Superman modeled after Barack Obama. And in the real world, Obama-as-Superman was a popular motif; "44" was reprinted on unofficial street T-shirts in a classic shirt-ripping Superman pose with an O on his chest.

The legacy of Priest's, McDuffie's and Milestone's efforts can be seen in today's Black comic book stories. A common theme that they share is an insularity—read Ta-Nehisi Coates's 2016 *Black Panther* run or Roxane Gay's *World of Wakanda* work during the same period, and one of the things you're struck with is how much more intimate these Black Panther stories are when they scalpel out and eschew the wider Marvel Universe context.

These aren't titles or stories that lean on, or are obligated to tap into, cameos from Captain America, Wolverine or Spider-Man to justify their importance.

From 2016 onward, the pivot towards a more Black-centered storytelling—where Black characters are allowed to frolic, develop, experiment and grow outside of typical publishing confines—was the vibe that defined Black comics in that era. N.K. Jemisin's *Far Sector*, for example, an off-Earth adventure starring Jo Mullein as the first-ever Black female Green Lantern, shows Jemisin isn't concerned with the established male Green Lanterns or all the cultural weight that comes with them. And in keeping with the cultural reactions of the times, after being teased in interviews and announcements, Milestone Comics returned by way of publisher DC Comics in . . . 2020.

That intertwining of Black writers' identities with their creations seems to be a vital part of graphic novel ingenuity. Under their pens, these characters take on a texture that eludes those of other writers. The creative freedom that comes with building a character and a world allows for explorations that are genuinely more unique and daring, even when writers might have to bump against the conventional established boundaries like Jemisin did when writing *Far Sector*.

Far Sector is just one such Black creative project that utilizes identity, context and time to tell better stories. Writer Matt Johnson's noir-styled graphic novel *Incognegro* is a series that reveals America's complicated racial history through the eyes of a biracial, white-presenting Black journalist named Zane, whose "superpower" is "passing," as he uncovers Jim Crow lynchings in the American South during the 1930s.

Yvan Alagbé is a French Beninese artist whose 2018 black-and-white French-language graphic novel *Yellow Negroes and Other Imaginary Creatures* is a volume journaling the Black immigrant experience in France during the 1980s. *Yellow Negroes* consists of humanity-centered stories of the Other through exploring a small set of characters—some Black, some white—as they navigate employment, housing, romance, sex work, displacement, police brutality and prejudice. Through Alagbé's panel composition and drawings, dialogue and narration, *Yellow Negroes* is an honest, pensive and sometimes biting look at the complications of class, race and citizenship issues. Alagbé's pencils place you in a world with blurred lines; the characters and settings are sometimes as indistinguishable from each other as the real-world proximity and entanglement found when people are living in the projects together. For me, his stylistic approach is a political statement about how arbitrarily the lines are drawn in real life when people attempt to unfairly differentiate their lives and fates from those of other people, and use those false distinctions to justify dehumanizing others.

What unites all of these stories are the Black artists and creatives who are able to create experiences where the stakes feel both real and human. Reading them challenges a lot of conventional representations of Black characters in graphic novels because they do not rely on their characters' impervious bodies like those of *Strange Fruit*'s Colossus, Marvel's Luke Cage or DC's Cyborg, or perfect intellectual, professional or class backgrounds like those of Black Panther, Hardware, Steel and others. Instead, their genius lies in positioning their characters to navigate settings, situations and foreign environments by fighting back to the center of humanity for themselves or others after being reduced to subhuman or one-dimensional in various ways.

For over sixty years, Marvel has published X-Men comics, and for over sixty years a big part of the X-Men's story has been the Black struggle. The X-Men have stood in for Black folks' striving for acceptance and integration, with the ideological nemeses Professor X and Magneto even being framed as an "MLK vs. Malcolm" opposition. And some of the comic's biggest storylines have dealt with situations that feel familiar to those of us with Black Paranoia and vigilance; the X-Men have watched viral assaults on mutants, had politicians attempt to legislate away their existence, seen vigilante hate-groups form to wipe them out, and continually had their existence culturally and literally policed. They've been experimented on, mined and exploited for their talents, and had parts of their bodies harvested, examined and sold. They've been enslaved and hunted, and created their own school and communities. The X-Men are guarded against having their population wiped out and are fiercely future-oriented; there have been decades of storylines and characters trying to prevent and anticipate the worst futures or timelines. These are, essentially, Black storylines and experiences, and an added element to it all is the existential "otherness" of their stories and characters that has intoxicated so many Black—especially Black and queer—people.

What's also true, though, is that in that same sixty-year history, no Black writer has ever written any of the core X-Men titles. Ever. In six decades and counting. Never. There have been Black pencilers like Larry Stroman and Eric Battle, who've worked on X-titles, and there've been Black writers on ancillary X-Men titles like Eric Jerome Dickey's *Storm* miniseries, or the recent *Bishop: War College* miniseries by J. Holtham. But these are also a familiar pattern of what we've largely talked about, too: short-term Black projects that give the company the sheen of diversity without influencing the core canon.

To be clear, the mainstream comic book industry continues to have a woeful diversity problem. There remain painfully few Black writers in the medium, and most often the ones that are awarded visibility are already on the higher end of visibility themselves. While there's been a burst of Black talent contributing to the likes of Marvel, DC and Image comics, they have still often trended as safer bets to helm titles: Roxane Gay, Ta-Nehisi Coates, John Ridley, Eve Ewing are, respective to their stature, better-known commodities with solid track records and built in audiences. That's not to take a single thing away from any of them, but it does point towards the limitations of what these corporations seem to understand when we call for diversifying their creators. Instead of fostering Black talent within their companies they prefer to go with a sure bet. As progressive as they've wanted to appear, the industry remains conservative at the end of the day.

Proof of our fantastic imaginations is routinely on display for publishers and creatives to see. Go to any comic book convention and you'll not only see scores of Black people dressed as popular anime, manga, sci-fi and comic book characters, you'll see how much we can take these concepts and reimagine and augment them. In some instances, it's our ability to amalgamize characters; people making DIY costume mash-ups of, like, Hellboy and Wolverine, or gender-bending and updating the look of Batman by also crossing him with Robin. But a lot of times, it's the spectacularity of Black women taking character designs and adding details to costumes or working in their equally imaginative approach to their hair. I saw one picture of a Black woman dressed as Poison Ivy and admired the way that she interwove a bushel of flowers into the configuration of her already styled burnt-orange hair. Or the brother at the New York Comic Con whose rendition of DC's Cyborg gave the character a more consistent and dignified look with his black-sleeved armaments.

One of my favorites was a sister who redesigned the Spider-Man villain Venom's costume as a sort of gothic ballgown, turning his teeth and tongue into a train on the dress.

I mention these examples not just to describe the costume ingenuity, but also because I have a hunch. I bet that if I close my eyes and put myself in these people's shoes, I can imagine a story in a story, just like when I'd sit in class or lay on my couch or hang out in Sean's basement and pull out a pad and start sketching popular or self-created superheroes. I bet that these fans, just like me, had a vision, had these wild, exhilarating takes about what their version of Poison Ivy, Cyborg, Superman, Venom, One-Punch Man and others would say and do and where they would go if they were the ones telling the story for once. I read a lot of comic book professionals' interviews, and it probably won't surprise you to hear that nine times out of ten, most of them talk about having been a fan or growing up reading the comic book that they're now writing. When I think about what Evans opened up for us back in 1947, I think of "Open the Door, Richard," the jukebox song playing in the opening scene of "Ace Harlem." When it was performed back in the day, it was a part of a vaudeville act where a Black drunk tried to find all these ways through an imaginary closed door. Who knew that would capture what so many of us experience telling our stories in the comic book world? With the genius dawn of *All-Negro*, Evans created a portal for us to step through. It might've closed on

All-Negro soon after it debuted, but the long tail of Evans's creation ushered in and contributed to a new cultural lane for Black people in popular culture. Decades after Lion Man and Ace Harlem came Black Panther and Luke Cage, and with them the influx of Black characters and creatives. It's been so, so much since 1947, so much ground has been made. But we've still got so far to go.

In the present, "Open the Door, Richard" somehow feels as relevant as ever. In so many of the major mainstream publishing circles, Black folks are still trying to break into the comic book world only to find the door completely shut. There's a seemingly invisible way into an industry that loves to move the knob around.

CHAPTER 2

Streemal

Navigating America's Education

Me onstage at the Education Leaders of Color 2019 National Convening. Photo courtesy of Satsun Photography.

> *I got, I got, I got, I got*
> *Loyalty, got royalty inside my DNA*
> —Kendrick Lamar, "DNA."

E ducation is supposed to be the door to a better life and set of opportunities, but too often the American education system smothers and smooths over Black genius. And in the process, our education system crushes and overlooks those of us who manage to use a series of academic, cultural and interpersonal brilliance to navigate the typical school settings and still thrive against the odds. Most of the time, schools, educators and families consider kids to be academic geniuses based on straight A's, high SAT scores and getting into elite high schools, colleges and universities. And those *are* genius markers, but there's *also* the ingenuity of genius that flies under the radar and doesn't look as obvious. It's a Black genius that has to understand tricky academic, social and cultural terrain in a bunch of different circumstances and basically create a DIY life curriculum to make it through.

I want this Black genius celebrated as well; the kind of Black students who find a way through a complex series of relationship negotiation, academic risk-taking, cultural creation and imagination. In my family, one of the geniuses, my uncle Alan, tried to define this sort of genius by telling people how he made it from deep Trenton to the University of Pennsylvania. As an educator, my years working in nonprofits and at schools forced me to reconcile how often I was being coaxed to value a limited definition of genius, and how that work sometimes made me lose my sense of authenticity, integrity and awareness of the world around me. For me, the beginning of those epiphanies came on the biggest stage at the worst possible time.

My uncle Alan went through a social-academic baptism by fire. He grew up the youngest of three siblings in 1960s Trenton and was the last child in my grandparents' house, my dad Wayne and my aunt Debbie both having left while he was still growing up. As a Black kid growing up in deep Trenton the closest school was Stokes Elementary. Not that he was there all that long; his boredom and acting out became proof that my uncle often outpaced everyone around him. Eventually, though, he convinced Nana to let him transfer to Princeton Day School, the nearby posh private school that offered him a scholarship. At Princeton Day School, he sat next to kids who came from the Gallup, Packard and Johnson (of Johnson & Johnson) families. And while that scholarship got him in, it didn't make him an insider at PDS; at first, the school placed him academically at the bottom of their classes. His second week there, a white boy called him "nigger" to his face.

Alan spent six years—sixth grade to twelfth grade—moving back and forth between two worlds: my grandparents' brick row-home in Trenton and the sprawling campus of PDS. Looking back on that time nowadays, he tells me how he started realizing that he was "never quite fitting in either one" anymore; when he went to birthday parties at their mansion houses, his classmates talked about going to Aspen and Vail for spring breaks. Even though he tried to hang, the reality was that he stuck out in all kinds of ways; they all dressed in bespoke suits and fancy dresses while he showed up in whatever leisure suits Nana felt they could afford. And while they all blended in seamlessly with each other at those parties, he would sometimes get confused for the staff by some of his classmates' family members. You'd think that being back home in Trenton should've been easier, but he started finding that people on the block saw him as some kind of snooty, smartass (to be fair, he is a smartass) brother too good to relate to anymore.

Still, the mixture of social and academic settings and conversations must've been heady for a Trenton kid feeling more out of place wherever he went. In 1968, when downtown Trenton was full MLK-assassination riots and razing, he was a fourth grader at Stokes still, and two years later he'd be at PDS, where the kids there probably looked at him like a looter.

The other thing that happened, though, was that swinging between Princeton and Trenton really opened his eyes to how lopsided and unfair things were depending on whether you were Black and poor or white and not poor. And that also meant that he'd have to quickly, and largely on his own, figure out how to do well in school and keep the peace at school (you can't body-slam in return every kid who's going to call you "nigger" and not eventually end up back at Stokes) as well as when he was back home in the hood. He had to figure out what to do with all the anger that started roiling in him as he got to be more aware of what was being taught at PDS and how that matched with what he was seeing and living in Trenton every day; the kind of place where his pop was shot in the back working a late night at the local grocery store. The Gallup kids wouldn't know anything about that, while the kids back around the way probably did. Hell, Trenton's so small they maybe directly or indirectly even knew the young guys that did it.

When he graduated from PDS in 1977 at the top of his class, he turned down an early admission to Princeton University to go to the University of Pennsylvania instead after seeing the Penn Relays on a trip to Philly. By then, the cultural whiplash between PDS and Trenton had given him a lot to think about, and only in the last couple of years did I come to understand what it was like for him.

"Growing up between two worlds (Trenton and Princeton) was not fun and cost socially in both worlds for years, not totally fitting in either one."

And if there's an origin story for his attitude and a temper that cooled way down in his sixties, it's from this time where the weight of those two worlds meant he developed an "attitude as self-defense [due] to not feeling adequate to either world or my family." And thinking about what it took to both succeed and survive, he turned it into a college senior paper where he put a name to what he had discovered. He called it "streemal educa-tion" (*formal* and *street*); a combination of what he learned growing up in Black Trenton and the white elite spaces like PDS and UPenn.

And while it might sound like code-switching, Alan saw streemal differently. Streemal is about melding street education and formal education into an awareness that "opens your eyes to the many inconsistencies of life and makes you scary to a lot of White folks." I really think what he's talking about is an earlier coinage of something similar to being woke, and all that really made my uncle was an unsigned rapper. He didn't have the beats or rhymes, but he knew the life: He'd grown up in Trenton and gone to private school in Princeton on a scholarship and to UPenn at a time when the university had only 350 Black stu-dents total. And he had stories on stories to intertwine with his domestic and global views. Freshman year at UPenn, he was in a small riot after a drunk white girl hanging with a group of white boys called Alan and the other Black guys he was with "a bunch of niggers." He avoided getting implicated by hiding out in the room of his "cool RA," who covered for him.

Riots stayed following my uncle after college. After he be-came a corrections officer for the New Jersey prison system, he'd tell us stories over family holiday dinners about people starting riots and prison breaks, and all the underbelly things like fights, affairs, mobs and drug trafficking.

And then he'd be able to take all that—all the crazy shit that was happening in Trenton, in prisons, in schools when he started substituting years later—and still be able to draw all these parallels to geopolitical and historical issues to help us see how many things that didn't seem to be connected, were.

And he knew how to do it in a way that shocked white folks and made them uncomfortable. Especially white folks who looked at him and where he came from, and thought that he'd maybe been let into places like PDS and UPenn out of pity. One of his favorite things in life to this day is to surprise people with how much he knows, how sharp he is and how much he realizes that you're probably underestimating him.

Alan developed the kind of Black cultural woke genius—what he considered streemal—that reminds me of conscious rappers. He knows how to seamlessly blend hood politics, street knowledge and academia. And he knows how to play it back in white people's faces, with conversations that would freak them out with his combination of know-how and Trenton slick-dude looks. He has the pedigree to back his thoughts up and would share the ways he was able to parse the world without a single hitch in his voice or his delivery.

That's why streemal isn't code-switching, because with code-switching you kinda flip one part of yourself to adjust to a situation. You upspeak when you maybe don't normally in order to be heard. You drawl your voice for dramatic effect to seem familiar with people; you whiten your voice to sound "more intelligent." My uncle, Alan Johnson, for right or wrong, has a genius that looked at that switch and snatched it off the wall. Tossed it away. This is a man who unconsciously snorts when he talks, might hitch at his dick while he's making a point, will casually toss in a "fuck" here or a "bullshit" there. A man who believes that anything other than his truth is a lie, that he is the embodiment in our family of "keeping it real." He has not been interested in playing the code-switch game that he's seen his siblings, and maybe even me, his nephew, sometimes play. To this day, he's someone who sees no value in switching up how people see him, hear him or experience him. I'm saying that my uncle Alan's genius after all those years where he couldn't make niggas in Trenton happy, or them white folks at PDS or UPenn happy, is that he chose to make himself happy. And fuller. And honest. He never stopped being afraid to talk how he talks, with all the knowledge that he holds. I'm saying that what keeps his genius in place are the same things that could have also kept his career in place—he's worked in prisons, at youth programs, been a substitute teacher—each time needing to switch up for some reason or another, but nine times out of ten it came down to one, and that's his *authenticity*.

For good or bad he's always been quick to call out bullshit—and then intellectualize about where your bullshit came from, who influenced you to be on that bullshit, and why you think your bullshit is working for you, but how thinking that's the case is total bullshit.

I love this man, who drives us crazy at dinner tables, who is still ready to throw ten knuckles up, who can carry a Jack Daniel's buzz and an electoral college conversation, who has an informed opinion on *everything* and may not always be right but is always hella clear and compelling. He's taught me so much (you hear that, Unc?), not just about merging and not modulating my voice, or that keeping it real is not just a hood flex but a way of living, but also that the cultural and intellectual compartmentalization may get them to like us but won't make them respect us or value us for everything we really, truly have to offer. He's shown me how to speak without weighing a myriad of microcultural calculations that might get you to forget, malform or hide your truth.

My uncle Alan is streemal, which is to say sitting in his genius right there in your face with no question. Trenton can only claim one hip-hop group—Poor Righteous Teachers, a late '80s to early '90s conscious rap group led by Wise Intelligent. Alan's a poor righteous teacher. He's my wise intelligent uncle whose genius can be seen as the genius of not watching one's mouth.

But I won't want him to, either.

I'd learn about another type of Black genius through my friendship with Jamil once I moved to Philly. I'd known Jamil for sixteen years before he died in 2022. We met hanging out at kickball games and The Attic hip-hop parties that Jamil and some friends of ours hosted in the upstairs space of the South Street punk bar Tattooed Mom under the group name Get Free Movement. The GFM's hip-hop parties were aimed at preserving the music's culture of joy, community, love and awareness, and as the emcee, Jamil ended each party freestyling for the crowd of backpackers, B-boys and B-girls, alternative kids and preppy folks, who rested their sweaty, weary bodies against the graffiti-covered walls or sat in one of the repurposed carnival bumper cars for their verbal nightcap.

Outside The Attic, Jamil was a human Swiss Army knife of odd jobs and hobbies. He taught himself to build houses and soup up Mini Coopers that he'd take joyriding around the city and down I-95. And with his passion for music and social issues, he adjuncted classes at his alma mater Temple and worked with our friend Jay in the BeatLab at Chestnut Hill College, where the two of them helped undergrad kids create their own socially conscious bars about the outside world and how it kept them out. As if that wasn't enough, the man did commercials; sometimes when I was sitting on my couch watching TV, suddenly Jamil's face would pop up in Channel 6 Action News, Mountain Dew, Maryland tourism or local small business commercials. His mind and his body seemed like they needed to be anywhere and everywhere. He was ubiquity in a human form, creativity in a friendly form. Just a whirlwind of energy and art.

When the GFM parties ran their course, we stayed in touch

through texts and DMs, which was how I also knew sometimes he was haunted by things, too. "Trying to be bigger than my challenges!" he DM'ed me once during a catch-up. A writer himself, he'd send me sprawling rap verses he was working on; elaborate, labyrinthine wordplay in Black Thought–like bars. Inside of them would be hurt, anger, frustration at the world, begging people to wake up. To see and be aware of the ways we were being controlled.

In June 2020 we checked in to see how we were both holding up during the Floyd-hot pandemic. Back then, he told me, "I'm having a feeling something like what the old slaves must have had after a lifetime of watching people killed that looked like them; that a war was being fought that might set them free." Jamil desired to be free, and sometimes I just knew by looking at his face that there were things that haunted him. "I'm trying to write out forty years of hate crimes and other physical/mental/emotional abuses," he wrote to me one time, "while caring for a ten-year-old daughter."

It was through writing to each other that I also learned where a lot of Jamil's pains came from. Like Alan, Jamil found himself immersed in a new, white world where he had to develop social and academic tools to survive as a preteen. Born in Camden, New Jersey, he moved with his family to the Philly suburban town of King of Prussia in the 1980s just after it had recently desegregated. Jamil's family, the McNeals, were one of the ten

Black families that lived in the town. The move came with "no direction. No preparation," he wrote, and all around them they saw the signs of the hostile territory they found themselves in. Doors down from the McNeals, a white neighbor's home had an open garage door with a Confederate flag hanging on the wall as "unashamed advertisement."

It was just as subtly hostile in school settings. In class and hallways and on the bus, Jamil faced endless ignorance and antagonism as a Black boy who walked around cloaked in Black-centric clothing, and came across as smarter than a lot of the other kids around him. As he swam the King of Prussia public school currents, his mind never forgot the things he learned in the McNeals' home library, Black historical books reminding him of what our people had and continue to go through.

Jamil's classmates were a collection of the maliciously oblivious and the dangerously ignorant. Like Alan, he ducked and dodged the verbal punches of being called "nigger" routinely. Some of the kids at school were skinheads, and the ones that weren't had parents and social groups that didn't care to know much about Black people and had limited exposure to anyone who didn't look like them. Caught between the ignorant and the incensed, he tried to fit in where he could to survive. "Your personality gets crafted by what you have to do, not what you want to do.

"I became the embodiment of a pop culture trope . . . [as] the anonymous Black friend of all the cartoon characters," he wrote. "You know you don't want to be lonely, so you listen to their music. You wear their clothes. You talk their talk, though it has a hard and bitter taste some days." Maybe the roughest thing he faced was the time he punched a white girl who called him "nigger" on the bus. As she was the sister of one of the skinhead boys also on the bus, the group chased Jamil and his brother home, standing outside the McNeals' house "banging on the front, back and basement doors" until Jamil called his mother, who eventually showed up with the cops and one of their uncles who lived nearby. Years later, Jamil contacted the white girl through Myspace in order to "rinse the trauma." She replied saying that she was "in a bad place" at that time and "didn't remember the moment at all."

Neither Alan nor Jamil saw the value of code-switching. Instead, Jamil found power in leveraging culture, intelligence and politics on his terms. In school he wore pro-Black and Afrocentric T-shirts and hoodies. One of his favorites was a shirt his dad had brought back for Jamil from his trip to South Africa to cover Mandela's imprisonment. The shirt was black, with an outline of the African continent in green. At the southernmost point, a man is behind bars. Lower and to the right were the words "Apartheid is slavery." His dad rode around in a bright red truck that had a bumper sticker with the word "amandla" in big, Pep Boys–style letters. When his classmates wanted to talk about

Transformers and skateboarding, that was fine, he could do that, too, but he would eventually spin the conversation around to the kind of political topics and social dynamics that they talked about at home—apartheid, American racism and how dangerous it felt to be Black in their own town and school. With friends, a mix of Black and white kids, he both talked about and observed what it took to fit in, to feel some sort of safety and social acceptance.

Jamil was tall, even at ten, and Black, and brainy and socially awkward and geeky at times, and I'm sure all of that put together resulted in a mixture of people ogling, adoring and being angry at him. He had to learn how to be nimble about where and how he fit in, but a lot of times he came back to the irresistible beauty of being himself. If there's something that I'd come to know, love and admire about Jamil, it was his inability to be anyone but himself. For a lot of us Black kids in similar predominantly white classes and schools growing up, code-switching wasn't even a conscious calculation; we just knew that if you were going to get along you had to make sure you sounded like the most palatable version of yourself so white folks would feel comfortable around you. About forty-five minutes away from him, I was flailing in a similar situation, navigating mostly white classes and trying to figure out how to shrink and protect myself so I wouldn't be too bullied by either the white kids I spent all day with in class or the Black kids on the bus when the school day was over. For me, changing parts of myself felt like a fair trade-off, because we weren't a race-talking, pro-Black family most of the time. Really, that didn't change for us until O. J.'s trial.

In the meantime, I found myself constantly trying on different personas and clothing in an attempt to figure out who I was, not to myself but to other people. I wasn't happy about code-switching, but I also didn't have anything around me telling me how to do things differently.

Jamil saw it differently: "Calling it code-switching assumes some control on my part, some way to not assume your favorite pantomime of me and draw the right response.

"I realized," he said, "[when] I was no longer forced to bend the way they did, when success was unbraided from whiteness, I started to craft culture." For Jamil, that's a power that came from blending together a sense of Black history and awareness, navigation of cultural landmines, emotional fluency, self-love and pride.

Once I started working in education, I realized how hard it was for people to acknowledge all the little Black geniuses in schools. I felt like you had to speak the same code as these kids, and if you didn't, you had to understand what you were looking for when it wasn't obvious, right in your face. I'd go to a lot of schools representing programs that were looking for the "diamonds in the rough," kids who floated above whatever flotsam surrounded them. Or they were called "the best of the best" or "college-going," and for a lot of programs that meant trying to find the at-risk kids who were the least risky. When I worked at a small charter school as a student recruitment director, I was charged to find and recruit only the kids with good grades—anything above a C—from all the "bad" public schools. But when I went to these schools with my stump speech about why rising high school freshmen should apply to our little charter school, talking to kids face-to-face, seeing what some Philly public school kids navigated every day, like schools with dripping pools of water in the middle of the hallway, I started realizing that the genius kids weren't just the ones expressing book smarts and good grades—they maybe didn't even *have* good grades. They were the kids who could read the cultural algorithm in front of them and find a way. The ones who, once you sat down and talked to them, would just casually tell you that a normal day for them was getting up and fixing breakfast for their siblings, maybe needing to walk them to their elementary school before they doubled back and got to school themselves. The ones who got through the school day and put up with being told that they were "not engaged," or maybe they were engaged—they could have all, some or none of their homework done, but more important, they could tell you about how they did or didn't get to it when they got home after they'd helped their little brother or sister with their homework and fixed everyone something to eat.

These were kids who were sometimes quiet in class but hyperliterate in the digital world, who'd found that online they could be cultural experts and leaders by out-knowing other kids on anime like *Cowboy Bebop*, *Inuyasha* and *Bleach* or creating mixes on YouTube and SoundCloud of their own beats, making their own tracks. They were the kids like Max and me sitting in class looking like we weren't paying attention because we were doodling superheroes, when in reality that was the best way to learn in classes so low in rigor you could put your brain on autopilot.

So I was often looking for the young Black geniuses who weren't just the obvious ones but the misfit ones, too. The ones who didn't have as much time as everyone else and were still making it work in school. They might've shown up with B or C grades but had A+ curiosity and social skills and the ability to think on their feet. I knew that those kids were always good for it, because they already understood how to balance the scales of priority and knew how to do just the right amount of everything—stay just beneath other kids' radar, participate at least when called on, read what you gave them but stayed reading things that they picked out on their own. Geeky without being A+ geeky, savvy without making others feel stupid.

It took me a while to detach myself from other people's, schools' and organizations' beliefs about who among these kids had a right to be seen and celebrated. It took even longer for me to realize that those sorts of messages spoke to a bigger picture. I noticed a tendency to dismiss the everyday ingenuity that surrounded us, how inside these Black communities, people's schools and households had often cracked the code for living under harsh, sometimes shitty conditions. Instead, we convinced families not only that their children's futures were bound to be poor, but also that if they really wanted to change that outcome, if they really cared about their kids, they'd do school lotteries and jump through insane hoops to give their kids a better shot.

But when I finally understood, I opened my mouth and let out a stream of Black manifestation that had been held in for too long.

✧ ✧ ✧

From 2006 to 2012 I developed my streemal through a mix of things. I took walks with coworkers to Kensington corner stores where we'd buy greasy breakfast sandwiches and fried chicken. I rode on the El and talked with elderly Chinese folks as they leaned on their rolling carts, sat at trendy gastropubs next to downtown white folks, went to church events and block parties with Black folks, sat in the back of a North Philly Catholic school classroom while Filipino and Latino kids shared soft pretzels and how to cuss in their languages. I went everywhere: dive bars and school board meetings, Freedom School meetings and mayoral candidate meetings. I learned about the city getting dressed down by activists like Mama Gail and passionate Black public-school principals. When I was going around town in my Teach for America job finding school placements for new incoming teachers, I once sat across from a principal who told me, "The problem is that some of these boys here are too busy trying to be girls." When I recruited at public schools, I had to talk about racism, religion, sex, gender, street life and poverty on the spot—sometimes all in the same conversation. I learned to clown people and be clowned; I got called "white boy" by Black central office administrators who found my tight pants and gingham shirts too funny for a brother claiming to be from Trenton, New Jersey. I learned to laugh—at myself, at other people, at situations—and I learned when to shut the fuck up and when to let people know to back the fuck off.

When I wasn't in the streets, I was constantly reading briefs, articles and memos and talking to people about what I was seeing and thinking about the Philly area's education scene. I didn't believe in "picking a side" so it never occurred to me to develop anything other than a pure, wide view of what was going on. No "union vs. privatization." No "charter vs. traditional public school." No "choice vs. no choice." I just wanted to learn and understand it all.

By the time I became Teach for America Philadelphia's executive director around 2012, I was at the height of my streemal powers; I'd been to damn near every corner of the city, over one hundred schools, and knew scores of people in all walks of life.

Now as executive director, I sat at big tables in big kitchens inside even bigger houses to chat with rich white people about giving big money to Teach for America, code-switching in its grossest, finest fashion, telling them about growing up in Trenton, the bad Philly schools I'd been in, riding around the poor neighborhoods they'd never heard of. All in gingham shirts with rolled-up sleeves and cuffed tight pants. I'd sit down with them on their couch or outside at a sunny country club, and I'd mentally access my Black Stories folder and start flipping my fingers to the best stories that would guarantee a donor check.

I'd turn off pieces of myself in order to sit there and talk and listen to them, which was sometimes so shameful and embarrassing, thinking about how I was not sharing what it was like needing to spit out all these stories while leaving out what else I felt. How uncomfortable it was sitting in these big, white, fancy homes where sometimes I'd run into Black and Latino house staff, and we'd all look at each other wondering, How'd we end up here, anyway?

I couldn't talk about how these were the same kinds of houses we'd spend weekends driving around gawking at during

Christmastime, or how we'd drive right up to empty houses like this when they were for sale, peeking in their windows and talking about how we'd decorate them.

I couldn't talk about how the times I'd spent in towns and homes like this often meant getting followed by the cops or how the time that I got ice cream in a fancy Princeton shop, the white mom in front of me in line accused me of stealing her twenty-dollar bill that was actually sitting on the counter. There wasn't room for those stories, about how homes and towns and people like them drew an invisible line between them and us, and here I was sitting there sinking all of that down into my toes and curling it behind my soles.

As executive director, I was many things—fundraiser, manager, spokesperson, thought leader, convener—but situations like that didn't often make me feel Black.

When I was done, I'd hop in my little red Elantra and leave those homes—one had a driveway so wide that horses galloped and grazed on perfect grass pastures on either side of you—sometimes with huge checks in my breast pocket, feeling big, guilty lumps in my body while I replayed whatever conversation I had just had. Then I'd start my car back up and let my streemal blood recoagulate into place again.

I spent months feeling like this, living with the realization that my organization's method of raising millions of dollars made me unrecognizable to myself.

And then, wildly, I picked the most awkward time to gather myself back in my streemal.

In spring 2013 we decided to throw a gala to celebrate Teach for America Philly's tenth year in the city. Over 150 people were invited to gather at the Westin hotel in downtown Center City. It was going to be a family affair—local TFA alumni, donors, school leaders and partners were all invited. Even TFA's founder Wendy Kopp came; I chatted with her in her hotel room, floors above the banquet hall where the gala would take place that night.

"You have your speech ready?" she asked me before I left.

"You know it!" I chirped, tapping the breast pocket of my dark suit.

Each time I rehearsed before the dinner began—once in the hotel hallway with my chief of staff and another time on the banquet stage podium during a mic check—I kept noticing the Black hotel staff moving about, arranging their uniforms for the night or setting up the tables. A couple times, they paused and listened for a minute, maybe leaning against the wall or stopping as they buttoned up their white-collar dress shirts. In my head, I felt them be like, Who's this brother up there talking like a white boy? Each time that old feeling came back; the spirit of keeping it real, that streemal coagulation, was happening.

When the gala started, I was seated at the VIP table of board members, high-profile donors and leaders like Bill Hite, the new Philly schools superintendent. My actual seat was next to an elusive donor who was rumored to be primed for giving after he'd learned his family's wealth came through slave money. I slowed down my streemal to make small talk and keep practicing my speech in my head. Each time I talked, the words in my mouth had the tinny taste of blood.

My speech came after a series of video testimonials and other speeches. I was introduced by Wendy, who invited me to take the stage, and made my way to it through a wave of warm applause, weaving between tables, exchanging the occasional handshake, back slap or forearm grab with the crowd.

In front of the mic, though, as I cleared my throat and scanned the room, watching the Black hotel staff shuffling from table to table clearing plates and filling glasses in the dimly lit room, those stony guilt lumps blossomed in my body again. A mix of shame, sadness, disgust and confusion washed over me, and though it dissipated when the applause ended, each time I drew in my breath to start, the lines of my speech erased themselves in my head. When I leaned into the mic, I realized something: a clarity and a coolness had washed over me. It felt like I was onstage at a church revival—something about those lights, that stage, that scene, all those people I'd spent time gladhanding, program apologizing, money talking, school visiting, making fake friends and big enemies in education circles.

It was like it all came to me at once, breaking through and breaking me: Being executive director felt like code-switching on Red Bull. I was constantly switching modes, tones and voices, hyperresponsive to every audience I stood in front of—current teachers, former teachers, board members, school leaders, superintendents, city council people. But hardly ever Black kids and families, hardly ever back in the community. Standing there, I remembered how after I got the job, I suggested that once a month I spend time teaching or assistant teaching in a Philly classroom and was told it was an ineffective use of my time.

I started realizing that, in contrast, what was considered effective was turning the community and the classrooms into petri dishes for observation and examination. How so much of what I was sometimes effective at was upholding a program that took new teachers on "community walks" around Philly, or sometimes had me escort donors and funders to schools where we'd grin and talk to the teachers and Black and brown students and then sit in offices, big houses and country clubs lamenting them. I thought about how one-dimensional those aspects of the job were making my interactions with Black Philadelphians, kind of like the hotel waitstaff that night—helping to set the table for me to do my job and then fading into the background.

Suddenly, I saw all of that for the bullshit it was. It was for someone else, maybe, but not for me anymore. I thought about all the things that job made me repress about what I knew and felt: how much our schools were intentionally broken, how so many of us Black folks were making it against far heavier odds than most of the teachers we were bringing in to teach. How 15 percent of my time was spent on the phone or answering emails from parents complaining about how unfair it was that their grown-ass child was having to teach in some "poor, dysfunctional" school in North Philly.

How every year, during the first month of the school year, we had teachers quit—some walking out in the middle of a class, some leaving on a Friday and never coming back, some moving off the waitlist of a graduate program or getting a lucrative job offer.

How a favorite story was about a young teacher that had to be removed from the job because she snapped back to her class one day, "I'd rather eat a wet bag of dicks." Some of the most righteously angry teachers that I heard from in emails, ran into at restaurants or took out for coffee, would also be the most disengaged in the classroom. They were more interested in anthropologically using the chaos around them to fatten whatever they learned at their liberal arts college or to start working on their exit plan to study in a master's program once their time was over.

For the longest time the mantra was that TFA brought in the "best and the brightest," but in reality I found that some of the best and the brightest were the kids the teachers were in front of and the people around them, especially Black folks, who had nothing to do with the program. People who'd actually figured out ways to endure and hack parts of the system around them, the same one that seemed to defeat a lot of the people we were bringing in and spending way too much time hand-holding. These were teachers, college graduates, who often couldn't see the many amazing kids in their classrooms. These teachers and their parents were so invested in protecting their own little genius that everything around them seemed like a threat to it.

It really surprised people when I revealed that despite being the executive director, who was supposed to have "power" or "autonomy" in that job, I actually found the opposite to be true much of the time. Most especially when it came to having to feed my *actual* cultural politics through a positional sluice as the regional office leader. My *actual* thoughts on race, class, our experiences as Black people, capitalism and the numerous ways that I saw white apathy play out largely had to remain unspoken during most of my time in the role talking with the TFA community about how I saw education, economics and culture.

Some of those donors and program officers were white people old enough to have kids my age, and I often thought about how those kinds of kids had given me hell from childhood to my thirties. They were the rich kids on campus at the University of Maryland, the private school and Ivy kids who ended up teaching and working at TFA; sometimes they were part of the crews I found myself hanging with during my initial years in Philly.

They were the kids raised to know how to talk passionately about race and racism, attuned and sensitive to not being explicitly offensive, but who still enjoyed the pastime of retelling stories about working in Black communities, complete with Blaccents, or spending their nights "slumming it" in Black social spaces—clubs, bars, parties—and going home with brothers they hooked up with. They were the kids who skirted a lot of actual real intimacy with Black people but spoke with authority due to the combination of their smarts, background and just enough experience.

So at that mic, like I was in a sci-fi movie and had suddenly taken a pill or had some mental block removed, all these thoughts came undeniably rushing back. Suddenly, at the height of the TFA gala, in front of a crowd of about 150 people waiting for me to inspire them, my streemal came back.

I cleared my throat, adjusted the mic and opened my mouth.

"I want you to look at your dinner plates, and each time I tell you a statistic, I want you to imagine one less thing on your plate." I slowly ticked off stats that gave a sense of what life was like for all the Black folks who weren't in the room, the numbers that were probably familiar to a lot of the other folks in the room who peddled poverty stories over lunches, drinks and meetings.

And then, after spitting out those numbers, I gave them a final image: "Now imagine what's left on your plate. That's what we expect Black people in the city to live off."

I stepped off the stage to strained applause. Honestly, my memory goes blank after that: I don't remember sitting back down or the rest of the night. Even now when people mention that night and that speech to me, I can't remember anything more than that out-of-body feeling of wanting to poetically let out a series of thoughts and feelings that I had pushed down to my feet and spent the last year walking on. I don't think of it as anything but an undeniable rush of clarity.

In the summer of 2020 hundreds of Black educators and students publicly stepped into their streemal, too.

"We need your voice."

"You gonna help out with some of these accounts?"

"You're a writer; could use your help on this, Tre."

On the low, a bunch of Black folks were hitting me up through texts and social media. Something was happening; while some of us were marching and protesting in the streets, another cadre of Black folks in education—teachers, support staff, administrators, students, parents, partners—were creating a digital town hall sharing their stories and experiences about how they and other Black folks were being treated at schools, organizations and institutions around the country. This happened in the form of anonymous Instagram accounts, each one with the handle Black@[name of place]. Accounts like Black@TFA, Black@KIPP, Black@[NameYourElitePrivateSchool], Black@[SocialImpactNonprofit]—it seemed like virtually overnight, every organization, school and university was suddenly getting embarrassed and called out through these accounts, each one detailing anonymized stories about the horrible treatment of Black students, staff members and families inside these places. Their stories—Black kids being unfairly punished, white coworkers stealing and getting promoted, white leaders making racist comments but never being fired, families and communities getting called "ghetto"—were the kinds of stories I was familiar with from my own career.

In post after post across these accounts, people talked about how they saw the script flipped on them; how they were praised for opening up their hearts, their pain, their stories, and saw themselves valued for the authenticity, skills and passions that they brought to these spaces during these bloody periods when everyone was watching a string of Black people get murdered or brutalized, only to inevitably be shunted, forgotten or diminished, slid right back to the bottom, over time.

I understood the big anger driving this—these were Black folks who'd been tired of the cyclical lies, statements and professional development sessions after the deaths of Trayvon Martin, Philando Castile and Sandra Bland. They were tired of the town halls, the lip service, the hidden and forgotten histories and contributions Black folks had made. I know this was especially true for some of us who held what I called "Negro whisperer" jobs, roles with titles and responsibilities that made the person seem important but were really a trumped-up version of Black community engagement roles. These positions were toothless in actual influential power but vital in keeping the people who didn't want to deeply engage with us in power. It's hard when everyone keeps playing in your face—asking you to stand up, lead new initiatives and conversations, come to work on painful days when you've watched other Black people be slaughtered, humiliated or harassed in online videos. When you witness this violence only to step into places perpetuating similar harms, with the added sting of those enacting that harm asking you for answers.

During 2020 those kinds of stories came out again, just like they'd leaked out before in 2013 to 2016, and that once again created a familiar whiplash cycle. A lot of Black people opted out of their jobs and joined the DEI field to become the trainers, coaches, healers and strategists that they couldn't be in their organizations.

Ultimately, 2020 felt like a racial *Groundhog Day* for Black people, and the fact that it happened during a pandemic meant that creating these accounts was one of the only ways that some of us could safely, publicly, unapologetically tell our stories. I'd read those stories and see people who had sometimes been sitting on pain or insults for years. Things that had happened to them or others that had gone dismissed or disguised as something else for years. How they'd gone heads down to work, to school, to meetings, to performance reviews, to gala events and stages, to community meetings and classrooms, swallowing anti-Black bile for years and trying not to make a peep. It might've felt crass for everything to bubble up when it did in 2020, amid all kinds of suffering and when routine normalcy had gone out the window for everybody, but that was the sort of crude oil that people had needed for years to get out and show the world.

These years have continually reminded some of us what the cost has been of relying on the streemal we learned in school to get by. In those years, Jamil's life was up and down, and he'd appear and disappear for stretches at a time. When we talked privately, it was most often about the pains of identity and how intractably white schooling has seeped into our very DNA. We talked about the mixture of self-loathing and disassociation that came with growing up in schools in "only one" settings like we had; how lonely and futile it felt to try and explain to everyone from your Black friends and family to Black people you didn't even know why you "talked funny," "dressed like that," hung around white people, struggled to connect, could be isolated and quiet one moment and loud and gregarious the next. How something as ordinary as school could rewrite your code in ways that could take a lifetime to undo. I don't know if Jamil left because he did or didn't crack the code, but I think the lifelong effort of trying cracked him.

A year and a half after George Floyd's murder, *Abbott Elementary*, a sitcom about a group of students and teachers in a fictionalized traditional Philadelphia public school, debuted in December 2021. In *Abbott Elementary*'s universe, the school feels like it's held together by the last few squirts of Elmer's glue from the teacher's desk. Each week, the show subtly reinforces how hard, absurd and unromantic it is to be in a school every day, with everyone from the new and old teachers to the kids trading places on who feels more on the verge of exhaustion and quitting.

Abbott represents the heart of what happens in a lot of schools. Abbott is Harriet Ball's pop-culture successor: human, heart-based teachers who see every aspect of their students' lives. Ball is known in some urban education circles for helping to popularize a form of culturally responsive teaching that mixed Black culture and references with academic rigor, and for creating the type of classroom environment that helped the Black kids she taught understand themselves. Ball's classroom inspired and was xeroxed by Dave Levin and Mike Feinberg, the two TFA teachers who worked with her at a Houston elementary school in the early '90s. Levin and Feinberg would go on to create the KIPP charter schools, and a central part of their school models replicated what they saw in Ball's classrooms: love, culture, high expectations and rigor.

While you can imagine a lot of scenarios where things could go wrong at the school, it feels like a stretch to imagine there being a Black@AbbottElementary account during the next reckoning. Abbott echoes a lot of Black and non-Black urban teachers' experiences; working in a school is a game of inches won through a mixture of relationships, humility and understanding of when to step up and when to step back as a teacher.

But the show also spotlights how creativity is often nurtured in classrooms like Abbott every day, and the educators who are willing to cede the ground to their Black students and let them be quirky, playful, imaginative—it reminds me of the best classrooms that I've seen in places like DC, Camden and Philly. Classrooms and schools where people felt like a community together, where kids weren't so tightly fastened to rigid rules, where the adults treated and gave the students what they would want for their own children or for themselves as children.

Man, what I wouldn't give to have more time with Jamil to talk and laugh about what we both might be seeing in something like *Abbott Elementary*. We would discuss the genius of how the show makes the school look and feel like a giant imaginarium, a lab where kids and teachers can joyfully run amok and get better through the mess of discovery together. I bet Jamil and I would've been able to rap about our years in classrooms both similar to and entirely different from Abbott; we'd be able to talk about the teachers who saw and saved us at times, or the moments when our quirk was strong enough to get us figuratively pushed to the corner of the room. I think more than anything else, we both would've eventually talked about how much we wished we'd spent our entire school years in such a place. That's what makes me the most wistful about the show: The school feels like a shrinking island, all that's left of the type of educational environment created for Black kids.

Years ago, over drinks, a Camden coworker listened to me talk about the kind of school I wanted to see Black kids thrive in. I described a school structure that was joyful, loving, free, abundant in creativity, deep in exploration, purposefully messy, focused heavily on developing a sense of identity and awareness of the world. He smirked over his drink and said, "You're a real Montessori guy, huh?" and I almost choked because my answer wasn't a school "type" so much as a school mindset. From kindergarten to sixth grade, my sister and I went to Bethany, a private Lutheran school in Trenton. Now, Bethany came with a lot of things—church service during the week, Monday morning attendance checks on whether you'd gone to church over the weekend, reciting whole verses of the Bible—but one of the biggest, most consistent things that we got there was a sense of pride in who we were, space to explore, individual attention to who we were becoming and a no-shame approach to who or where many of us came from. Bethany had a largely Black and white student population, and most of the teachers were white, but as Black kids a lot of us thrived because we had a strong mixture of play, practice and positivity (prayer, too, obviously). It wasn't until I went off to Ewing Public Schools that I almost immediately encountered the sort of negative attitudes that could crush Black kids. In Ewing, first at Fisher Middle School and then during my years at Ewing High, teachers and classmates constantly belittled how smart I was from the start, and the school tracking system automatically placed most of the Black kids in the lowest classes. A sort of rampant scarcity ran through those schools, where a lot of us Black kids were trying to figure out which teachers and classes we could trust to help us make something of ourselves once school tossed us out into the real world.

Overall, I wouldn't say those schools or school years had much love in them day to day; most of the time they felt like lukewarm warehouses preparing most of us to work at the General Motors plant down the road or go into one of the local trade businesses between Trenton, Lawrenceville and Hamilton. Around the start of my junior year, former Ewing High kids started showing up in the cafeteria during our lunch periods, decked out and looking smart and professional in military uniforms, driving in from where they trained in "faraway" places like Fort Dix, or somewhere in Michigan or Texas. One guy got our home number and called it daily for almost a week, leaving messages on our answering machine to see if I'd read any of the US military literature he'd given me, or maybe I'd like for him to stop by the house, or maybe we could go out for pizza. My mom caught a message one time and immediately deleted it. "You aren't ever calling him back," she said, "and the next time he's at the school, you tell him you aren't interested."

So schools like Abbott might as well be fiction in the real world. In our actual reality, time sadly remains an unbroken loop. My sister's youngest child, my nephew, goes to school in a nearby central Jersey district, where he's about to enter middle school. My nephew is such a special, creative kid. Since he was five or six he's been making DIY replicas from bits of things he finds around the house of everything from Ben 10 power bands made from toilet paper tubes to action figures made from pipe cleaners, and one time a fake Nintendo Switch.

My nephew lives for creativity. His school system lives for creative ways to squash it.

In school, he's fought an all-too-familiar battle for himself. His uniqueness is treated like a constant, "troubling" problem for his teachers to address, and in class and at recess he's teased and bullied by some of his white classmates where—like Alan, Jamil and me before him—he's in a place that's got way more white kids than Black kids. For the last couple of years now, this NJ school district has tried to place my nephew, one of the few Black boys in his grade, into their special education and needs program. Instead of being curious, and nurturing all the creative energy and ingenuity that we routinely see at home—that limitless series of ideas and inventions that he wants to try out, his drive to take things apart and put them together again and see not just how they work, but if they could also work differently—they want to exorcise it out of him. If he won't get with the program and comply, then he's clearly a problem that needs to be relegated to another part of the system. It doesn't matter that he's roughly a solid B student; he needs to understand that he's not a genius in their eyes but a glitch in their system, and that they've got fixes for glitches. They've repeatedly and disruptively called my sister at home and at work about their "concerns" about this soft-spoken, imaginative, brilliant Black child who loves Mega Man and *Back to the Future*.

Hanging on my fridge is a Spider-Man drawing he did for me on Christmas Day in 2021; we each drew a Spidey for each other while sitting at my Nana's dining room table. Each day when I reach for something in my fridge, I look at the drawing and am reminded that over in New Jersey, my nephew and my sister are locked in an endless but familiar battle for something as simple as keeping this boy's streemal. In the drawing, Spidey has one arm out, shooting an arc of black webbing that darts straight towards the edge of the paper and ends in a web. Sometimes I stop and look at it, staring at the tiny intricate, interlacing design of these threads that hold it all together, and imagine Alan, Jamil, me and so many other Black kids who have been stuck in America's educational web struggling to get out. When I close the door, it's with a grimace that a kid like my nephew is in that web now, too.

CHAPTER 3

Live Right, Do Right, Fight Like Hell

Family and Legacy

My Nana Marie Johnson sitting with B. B. King's band at a hotel in Florida. Photo courtesy of the Johnson family archive.

For a few minutes, Pop-Pop was Katie Couric–level famous. What else could I have thought? I was standing with my family, dressed in my good clothes, surrounded by screaming, happy people waving flags and sparklers, jumping up and down, cameras out, lined up on either side of the street right in the middle of downtown Trenton, New Jersey. It was 1996 and everyone was there waiting for the Olympic torch to pass through Trenton on its way to Atlanta for the '96 Olympics. Trenton! The place with the bridge with the saltiest message in big, lit but only half-working block letters: TRENTON MAKES THE WORLD TAKES. Trenton, where sad, shady people sat on schoolyard seesaws shooting up in the sunlight. Where every year everyone came downtown to eat, drink and conversate at the Heritage Days Festival. Trenton, where as a Friday night ritual we drove to the spot in a shack called Bud's and ordered fried shrimp and fries, cheesesteak and fries, wings fried hard and fries. Where Cadwalader Park had an underground bear cave. Trenton, the little overlooked city caught between Philly and NYC, where I'd get hyped telling people three things—that Dennis Rodman and *Who's the Boss?* star Judith Light were born here, and that once we were the country's capital.

And now, on a June evening, right after it had left Couric's fingers, the torch was making its way to my Pop-Pop's fingers. Famous. That's all I could think. Pop-Pop's famous. I watched

Trenton, NJ, 1996, when we all gathered to watch Pop-Pop Johnson receive the '96 Olympic torch. Photo courtesy of the Johnson family archive.

that little flame make its way down the street. Watched the crowd double up in energy, in screaming, watched that little flame get closer, get bigger, watched Pop-Pop get wheeled towards the center of the street to meet whoever was carrying the baton next. I watched the rest of the family step a bit closer in. Standing there watching that small torch waving its way down the lane, looking like a hot ice-cream cone, I remembered all the times in school I had to do family history assignments or interview people in my family; the times I had to try and figure out stories about who we were and what, if anything, made us special. Back then, it was so hard to get people to tell me stories about our family history besides some snippets about coming from the South and how long we'd been in the Trenton area.

Passing the torch

A Trenton pastor—Rev. Willie Smith—wrote an op-ed to The Times, *a local paper, about keeping Buddy Johnson as one of the '96 Olympic torchbearers despite his health condition.* Photo courtesy of the Johnson family archive.

For years I'd go around thinking that Pop-Pop Johnson and that Olympic torch moment was the only noteworthy thing to ever happen in our family. I started thinking that John "Buddy" Johnson, aka Pop-Pop Johnson, was the only blood avatar worth patterning myself after, a man known all around Trenton, who was connected and civic, who ran the local IGA grocery store down the street from my grandparents' house.

The crazy thing is that this all almost didn't happen. After he'd been picked to be a torchbearer, he had a brain aneurysm, which meant that he had to get around in a wheelchair. And because traditionally the Olympic torchbearers ran or jogged with the torch as part of the ceremony, the idea that my Pop-Pop wouldn't be able to do that because of something he had no control over made a lot of people in Trenton who respected and knew him nervous that he wouldn't get his moment.

The situation was up in the air enough that a week before the torch was set to pass through Trenton, Reverend Willie J. Smith wrote an op-ed in *The Times* testifying to my Pop-Pop's importance. He listed all the great things my Pop-Pop had done for the city; how he hit up local businesses to cover the rent for the city's citizen action center, a place where "local residents might find a listening ear for hearing about, and finding some resolution to, such issues as crime, home repair, violence, drug abuse or just trying to pay the rent." He talked about how Pop-Pop's work at the center included opening the door "to Alcoholics Anonymous and [holding] flea markets to raise funds." Reverend Smith also talked about how my Pop-Pop went to Philadelphia, where he learned about the idea of police and community mini-stations, where police and residents could address community concerns in hopefully better partnership together. As someone who was once held up and shot in the back while working late night at the IGA Food Market, he wanted to continue to figure out ways to better address what was going on around town.

That seemed like inspiration enough, maybe a good enough story for me to pin my future on.

But almost twenty years later, my Aunt Debbie, Nana and

Pop-Pop Johnson's oldest of three, would pass out a family photo album to each of us on Thanksgiving 2017. By then, Nana and Pop-Pop were gone; Pop-Pop had passed only a handful of months after holding the torch, and Nana a handful of months before that Thanksgiving in 2017. I flipped through my copy once I got home that night, sitting there and going through the photographs, the xeroxed copies of old certificates, obituaries, speeches and diplomas. I started thinking about the stories I'd heard growing up. In my ninth-grade term paper about Malcolm and Martin, I mentioned that Alice (Nana on my mom's side) had told me about taking a bus to hear Dr. King's "I Have a Dream" speech at the National Mall. From that night on, I wanted to be my own lil' Alex Haley, thirsty to figure out what other stories I could learn about my family.

That hunting didn't just put me on a path to understand who we were; along the way I figured out that the flickers of cultural, social and professional genius in my family were actually the keys to living a better, more liberated life.

When I look through the stories in my family's history that provide these blueprints, three people come to mind: my distant relative James Walker Hood Eason, and two of my grandparents, Marie Johnson and Robert Murphy. Each one has a story I want to sit around the table talking to my family about.

In the pursuit of chasing history, I found that my family members' lives had been leaving me gifts the whole time.

And it started with that Thanksgiving photo album gift. I pick it up all the time; it looks like a cheaply made manual or training guide for a mom-and-pop nonprofit. It's white with black spiral binding looping it together. Its plasticky cover and xeroxed pages immediately bend and droop like a wet lunch bag when you hold it up. On the outside, though, there's a picture: a computer-generated illustration of a tree with a mossy, sparkly green top and a thick, brown stem of a root. The trunk reads "2017" vertically. The roots are labeled with cities: Atlanta, Georgia; Trenton, New Jersey; Marion, South Carolina; Sunbury, North Carolina; Princeton, New Jersey; Cranford, New Jersey; New York, New York; Philadelphia, Pennsylvania; Gary, Indiana.

Five branches thread themselves into the tree's scalp, and each branch bears a name as you read it from left to right: "Glosson" and "Robinson" on the two leftmost branches; "Tyree" and "Johnson" on the right. Directly in line with "2017," the middle branch climbs up into the tree, and on that stem is the name "Eason."

Who James Walker Hood Eason was, where he came from, what his life consisted of, when he died and, most crucially, how and why he died, and whether it was important—knowing those ingredients of his life would help me understand how any sort of greatness could come out of our family. I wasn't sure if it was a fluke limited to only him and my Pop-Pop Johnson, or if there was actually a seed of it in every one of us. And not on some "we come from kings and queens" shit, but because growing up in Trenton felt like growing up in America, looking up from the bottom of a well. Not seeing anything or anyone else really rise up in or out of it made it seem like any Trenton fate was going to be about how to make the best life possible inside of Trenton. Not that that was bad, but when damn near everyone on both sides of your family are all in the area, the map—of America, of the tristate area, of the city, of life—feels really small, or maybe, like that's as big as it gets.

Based on where you look, Eason's birth and parentage are confusing; official 1880 and 1900 census reports and our family's oral history place James, born 1886 in Sunbury, North Carolina, somewhere in the middle of his father William Eason's brood of kids that numbered anywhere between six and ten. After his first wife, Parthenie, William Eason remarried and fathered additional children with his second wife, Louvina, and it seems they took in some young relatives. But all historical records seem incapable of pinpointing who James's birth mother was—Parthenie, Louvina or a woman named Martha Ballot, who is referred to as his mother in a family history I received from my aunt, while the online archive African American Registry's entry "James Walker Hood Eason, Activist Born" states that his mother's name was "Lucinda."

They throw an additional curveball by stating that his father's name was "Douglass."

As with many Black American lives in those early post-slavery years, James's history seems to exist somewhere between unclear documentation and word of mouth.

But if there was anything remarkable about James, it was his mouth. James graduated from Hood Theological Seminary in 1914, right at the start of World War I, and by the time the war ended, he'd cemented a reputation as a "flamboyant, silver-tongued" orator involved in activist groups and movements. A lot of this was spurred by the unyielding conditions that hadn't changed while Black folks were away fighting trench warfare—housing, education and job discrimination still existed, and racial violence kept a tight boundary against progress. After becoming a Philadelphian, James was disgusted with the local NAACP's response to the weeklong 1918 Philadelphia race riot that involved five thousand whites and Blacks fighting across a two-mile stretch in South Philly. The riot started when an angry mob of one hundred white Philadelphians stood outside the home of Adella Bond, a Black female probation officer who was the first Black homeowner on the block. They shouted and threw a stone through her window, and when Bond shot a bullet from her window to alert police, a riot ensued.

By the time the riot subsided, scores of Black homes had been ransacked and burned, and dozens of Black Philadelphians were either dead, tortured or hospitalized. In the riot's aftermath, many Blacks felt the NAACP were too disaffected and passive, so James Eason and other Black clergymen started the Colored Protective Association as a means of taking a more proactive approach to what was happening. Around this time, Eason also joined Marcus Garvey at the United Negro Improvement Association (UNIA) in 1919, eventually leading the Philadelphia chapter of the organization, whose mission was economic independence, Black nationalism and racial unity.

Eason was electric working with Garvey, making national speeches at rallies and events in support of UNIA's interests. He was impassioned by the idea of Black liberation and had no confidence in white America's progress towards accepting Blacks as equals. In time, Eason fully left the ministry to join Garvey's organization. In a way, it was Eason's own streemal moment; the riots and decaying American conditions, and the fecklessness of some of the other Black civic groups, catalyzed his whole being, and he found a new home and fuller identity through UNIA's work. By 1921 he'd raised nearly $1 million for Garvey, but the process of doing so seems to have raised some questions for Eason, too.

Because James Walker Hood Eason was killed on January 1, 1923, down south in New Orleans. He was shot, and three men were arrested in connection with his murder. The contentious belief is that Eason, after digging into Garvey's UNIA records, found enough financial improprieties and questions that he was willing to testify against his friend and leader. As a matter of fact, Eason used his silver-tongued skills to denounce Garvey and his association with Garvey a year before at the 1922 UNIA convention. No one knows for sure, but people have pointed the finger in every direction possible about who sent Esau Ramus, a Garvey acolyte who was "looking to impress" the leader, and William Shakespeare and Fred Dyer, both of whom were affiliates of Garvey's UNIA-based security force, to go to New Orleans and kill Eason in a blaze of bullets. James W—not John W, not Uncle Hood—died three days later in a local hospital, and it's said that on his deathbed, he named Garvey's revenge as the reason for the shooting. There's no proof, but he died all the same.

I learned about James Eason around 2020, a good seven years after I'd shown my ass giving that speech at the TFA gala and almost one hundred years after he'd been murdered in New Orleans. And I'm not saying that what we did or were doing was at the same scale—Eason was explicitly fighting for Black liberation, while I was, at best, tangentially helping to address it—but what does stick out to me is the idea that someone else in my family once publicly stood up for his beliefs and paid a consequence. My immediate family aren't the kind of people that I think of as risk-takers; most of us are concerned about making sure we keep our jobs and our homes. When I left my job as TFA executive director, I didn't talk about my final bow at the gala with my family—it felt like a story that they might see as reckless, scary, "not smart to do." We're more "head down" than "neck out," and so that moment of clarity for me that night felt right in the world but wrong in my family, so to speak.

I actually mostly felt that I had failed my family at that time—the idea of losing "a good job" and also making a scene with a rude speech felt to me like crossing something of a line of pride and dignity in my own family tree. TFA would be fine. Philly education would be fine. The rich donors and board members would be fine. But that choice made me wonder if I'd be OK, and if I'd be OK in my family's eyes. I think I felt like any greatness for our family lay in whether or not I had that job, despite the fact that the job came with the sort of endless bullshit from a variety of people around me that made it feel thankless. Still, I thought the best thing to do was to find a way to endure the job, which, ironically, was exactly what I watched a lot of Black people in and outside of my family do all the time. The job somehow felt like it was so important that I had to figure out a way to make it work, even as it burned and ate me up. Life had set a weird bar for excellence, and I was struggling to meet that bar for what was really someone else's purpose.

Maybe I hadn't come that far at all? That fall from the job made me wish that I'd been smart enough to have created or owned something myself. I wasn't the boss of anything at the end of the day; I was the latest replaceable steward for something that I wasn't sure I fully believed in once I saw it for all that it was. But back then, I also didn't know that Murphy's Bar had ever existed.

Murphy's Bar and Lounge was proof on my mom's side of the family that we could do things bigger than ourselves. The establishment was started by my Pop-Pop Robert (my mom's dad) and his younger brother Johnny, along with their father, my great-grandfather Edmund, who we called "Big Mommy's Pop-Pop" in reference to his wife, Mattie, aka "Big Mommy." The three Murphy men opened Murphy's Bar and Lounge in 1967, during a time when Trenton's business corridor was thriving with Black businesses. As a family with Jehovah's Witness DNA in our religious background, opening a bar seems kind of odd; never in my life have I ever seen Pop-Pop have a drink.

But the Murphy men, particularly my great-uncle Johnny, saw a chance to do business. Their idea for Murphy's Bar and Lounge was to fill a niche in the Black bar business, to be the kind of establishment that was more than a watering hole by offering classy entertainment. Their clientele was mostly Black, though they served white people, too.

The 1960s were a hard time to open a Black business, though. By that decade, Trenton had been on the back end of a large influx of Black folks from the Deep South, a lot of them drawn to the small metropolis feel of a city situated between Philly and Manhattan. And as they moved into town in droves—the largest wave coming in the 1950s—despite promises that the North would be better, most Southern Blacks moving to Trenton ran into the same clusterfuck of job, housing and social discrimination. And jobs were hard to come by, too; while Big Mommy's Pop-Pop worked at the General Motors plant and my Pop-Pop was working at Reedman's, most Black folks who migrated to Trenton were holding down low-wage, low-dignity jobs "as janitors or sweepers and outside the city as potato pickers, chicken pluckers, or part-time day laborers," as historian John T. Cumbler writes. A decade before my relatives opened Murphy's Bar and Lounge in 1958, the New Jersey Division Against Discrimination received almost one thousand complaints from non-white, mostly Black job seekers.

And while all that's unsettling, it makes it all the more amazing that the Murphys opened a bar with the vision of doing something different and "classier" for Black folks in town. It makes sense in hindsight; growing up, Pop-Pop always had a taste for finer, classy things. He bought the women in the family fur coats for Christmas, drove Lincoln Town Cars and loved to have nice furniture. Even his bathroom was stylish, with gold-toned faucets. And he was definitely someone who made a distinction among Black folks—he didn't like laziness, joblessness, fecklessness.

But you could see what the Murphys were going for. Trenton might've had bars, but it didn't necessarily have clubs, and Murphy's Bar and Lounge was trying to lean into the "lounge" end of things. I've seen pictures of my grandparents dressed up at Black NYC clubs at that time, the kind of places where you could dance to bands. Pop-Pop seemed to want Murphy's to have a similar feel. I don't think Murphy's was interested in just being another watering hole; more like something somewhere between upscale and dive that these three nondrinking men wouldn't mind being seen as customers of.

Their genius was seeing that there was a community and an opportunity to serve that community by giving them the kind of establishment that felt entertaining, dignified and approachable but Trenton at the same time. Back then, Trenton didn't have a lot of places offering that mix, and the city's segregation meant that if there were lounges and clubs that offered anything like that, not a lot of them catered to, or were owned by, Black folks.

Still, the bar seems like a funny, risky thing; it might've taken a second mortgage for them to purchase the space, which, even then, wasn't located in a great part of Trenton and didn't offer street parking.

Murphy's Bar was sometimes a mixed blessing for the Murphy men. The bar might've been cool, but it wasn't without its problems. There were incidents: One time, there was a shooting outside the bar. The license was almost permanently revoked when John Howard, a Murphy's regular, posed as a bartender there and unknowingly helped two undercover agents purchase a hooker. And, like a lot of Trenton bars, Murphy's had an issue with underage kids sneaking in for drinks.

There were bigger things, too, though, like the weeklong riot after MLK's assassination. In April 1968, over two hundred businesses suffered $7 million in damages as scores of Black Trentonians burned and looted Trenton's downtown. Nearly three hundred people—a combination of Black men and youth—were arrested for pillaging shops and fighting with police. Schools canceled classes, shops closed up and prayed for the best, and racial tensions boiled over so hard that downtown Trenton was a massive melee. And even though Murphy's Bar and Lounge was a mile away from the downtown, over on the 700 block of East State Street, it's still miraculous that the bar survived a riot that Trentonians today will tell you the Black Trenton commercial corridor never recovered from. Insurance companies stopped insuring Trenton businesses for a while, and some shops never reopened again, with a lot of commercial business shifting to outside the city.

The Murphy men weren't the type that fought—not that they didn't have problems with white people, too, or see the same things happening that other Black folks in Trenton and around were seeing. I'd be surprised if it turned out that they were anywhere near that '68 riot. Big Mommy's Pop-Pop already felt too old to be involved in running a bar, and Pop-Pop was holding down a day job and a household. He didn't take time off for much of anything—when I interviewed Nana for that school essay about Malcolm and Martin, she told me she skipped work and took a bus to DC to hear the "I Have a Dream" speech while Pop-Pop went to work.

I don't entirely know what that says about him, or about how he was raised. Unlike someone like Eason on my dad's side, the Murphy men seemed way more into a kind of respectability, the kind of respectable Pop-Pop was. He was also quick to refer to someone who didn't seem like he or she was doing anything with their life as a "nigger." I think of him enjoying small wins in life, beating the guys at work in the weekly NFL pool and for a short time playing in a bowling league with them. Hell, for all I know he might've felt his civil rights movement was making his way from the garage to the C-suite.

Not that it mattered. Four years later in April 1972, Murphy's Bar and Lounge had a fire. The official report, the one that ran in the local paper, said that the fire was caused by a "chimney defect" that started on the first floor, spread to the second and sprang to the third floor's cockloft. Firemen came and put the fire out, and it was treated as such a nonevent that the article went on to say the regulars went back into the bar "to continue their drinking." Not too long after that, though, the bar closed. If you go to the location nowadays, you'll find a Baptist church's parking lot flanked by rowhomes and an abandoned advertising company. Murphy's Bar and Lounge now exists only in photos and the occasional family conversation.

Still, it's the kind of story that I think our family is hungry for, and something that Black folks in general need to hear a lot. I loved how audacious Big Mommy's Pop-Pop, Pop-Pop and Uncle Johnny were; there's something very inspiring about that to me. It's not that they opened a bar/lounge; it's that they built something together in Trenton, during a stretch that was one of the city's shakiest times for Black people. The bar ended up being a financial failure of sorts—a bit before the fire, it fell into bankruptcy, and that accident became a double whammy—but the Murphy men still managed to do something special in the city for a few years. They lifted up Black Trenton—even a little bit—with their vision of creating the kind of place that you didn't have to walk into bowed or be barred from entering. And it worked for a good time; the bar was popular and hopping during its run, and there are family whispers about big names that played at the bar during its heyday. If you drive through Trenton now, you'd never believe that anything like Murphy's Bar and Lounge really existed; the city's been reduced to a kind of urban rubble after periods of rejuvenation. And just like that, Trentonians are right back to where we started—having to go elsewhere to rest and relax.

My two nanas' approaches to leisure and community have

helped me understand the importance of living as balanced a life as possible. Growing up, they both took AC (what Atlantic City is often called round the Jersey/Philly area) bus trips on Friday nights, a lot of times on a Friday payday. This was back in the '80s when AC's population and casino workforce was heavily Black. In the years before, AC had already started establishing itself as a sort of vacation or leisure place for Black folks in the area with the Black-only Chicken Bone Beach, and Black-owned hotels and businesses like Club Harlem. And once the casinos really started hitting in the 1970s, AC's appealing boardwalk and beach culture got even more attractive for us. Propping up the casino business was big business, so folks like my nanas— Marie Johnson and Alice Murphy—would take some dollars and some girlfriends and spend the evening out at AC casinos playing "the machines." This was especially easy when the casinos partnered with bus companies to bring people on round-trip rides to Atlantic City and back.

I have a lot of memories of them doing this, particularly Alice. I would sometimes ride with my mom to drop Nana Murphy at the parking lot where people would catch the almost two-hour bus ride to the boardwalk. She would go with her sister Aunt Tootie or someone from work, and they'd spend hours bopping between casinos. Same with my Nana Johnson (Marie), who also loved playing the slots. Both women were mothers, wives and workers who liked to dip out to AC and have their own adventures once the workweek was up. And these outings were different than the ways they usually went, where both households took their kids to the AC boardwalk in the '60s back when the planked promenade was a bit of a novelty. Families, particularly Black families, would stroll along the boardwalk decked out in their good clothes or casual summer clothes and take pictures.

But I love picturing Marie and Alice on these nights—part of the bus trip and railroad culture that many Black women started years before—strolling the same boardwalk, man- and kid-free, enjoying themselves with their girlfriends and taking in the ocean air, the viciously bright blinking casino lights, the constant bustle of people. Both of them saw the genius that came with rest and fun, carving out and taking time that was theirs, just being free, walking the boardwalk, smoking Salems, laughing with girlfriends from work. Neither of them, to my knowledge, played anything other than the slots—I don't think they were card game ladies—and I can picture them both sitting there at the machines with a bucket of quarters, laughing and chatting with their girlfriends about the week or their hopes of winning big and what they'd do with the money. These were lotto-playing, bingo-going women—both my nanas were big on picking the numbers they'd play or having us kids pick. They looked for significance in numbers like gambling numerologists. Birthdays, numbers that popped up frequently during the week in odd places, clock times, whatever. Their lives, their pastimes at firehouses and house parties playing games like Pokeno, seemed fixed in these social rituals that mixed gambling and girlfriends. And those Friday night AC bus trips were some real treats for them—a way to take all those things these Black women loved doing on the road somewhere where it was theirs and only theirs.

I mean, this was still post–MLK riots in Trenton, when the city was recovering mainly because a lot of Black folks didn't have the money to go anywhere else. People like my nanas were working good jobs, but hard jobs—Marie worked as a manager at the Tasty Food restaurant and was a supervisor at the New Jersey Motor Vehicle Commission downtown; Alice worked on the assembly lines at the General Motors plant and local warehouses like Campus Fundraisers, putting together cars and college care packages, respectively. These were the kinds of jobs that made your neck, your hands, your feet and your back tired. The jobs that came with all kinds of bullshit.

I know Alice—Nana Murphy—liked to smoke packs of Salems when I was growing up because I'd see her on her back patio tapping ashes into a tray while we sat on bright plastic furniture in the summer sun. I'm imagining her in the Tropicana or Harrah's sitting in a raised chair, dragging on a cigarette and laughing as she chatters with whoever is sitting next to her. I can see her dark, bright eyes twinkling, happy and open, not straining to make sure some mechanical bits were put in the right spot or that the right number of linens went into the box. I can see her dark, bright eyes gauging every slot pull, waiting to see the rows of fruits and face cards add up to some winning combination. I can see her dark, bright eyes as she gleefully cashes in her winnings and tucks them away in her purse—some for herself, some she'll claim were her overall winnings. And then maybe she steps out onto the boardwalk, maybe sneaks in another cigarette with her back to the casino, letting the ocean breeze catch the smoke and push it down the planks. I bet she still feels happy and relaxed and thrilled to be out with her sister and girlfriends from work for a night. So I like that they knew the rest of us would just deal on those Friday nights—nights when they didn't have to worry about how much pork chops and rice to make, cleaning up the house, listening to everyone else's day, fussing over the light bill, whatever. Those Friday nights at AC where she just got to be Alice—not Nana, not Mom, not wife, not cook.

I learned to appreciate why Nana needed those occasional AC nights after I worked a couple of summers with her at a warehouse in Ewing. At Campus Fundraisers, hourly workers opened up boxes of linens and towels and assembled them into care packages to be sent to college students. Nana worked the assembly line putting the packages together, and I worked in the back room breaking down cardboard boxes with a box cutter. Those were eight- or nine-hour days, and from the open bay door I'd be able to watch Nana rotely work putting care package after care package together. We'd ride both to and from work together in her silver-gray Mercury Cougar listening to Shaggy on cassette; when we climbed into the car after a day's work, we'd both be sweaty and dusty with cardboard. She'd get home and still have to cook dinner. I'd come home and wait for it.

My nanas shed all those things and stepped out for the night and maybe felt like millionaires before stepping back on the bus.

And Marie was big on stepping out, even around the country. Way I hear it, Nana Johnson was a boundless, insatiable, intrepid traveler. She and her best friend Ms. Marion saved up money and toured the country, from New York City to Vegas to California. Sometimes they traveled with a group called the Vagabond Travel Club, sometimes on their own. That's her pictured at the top of this chapter. The photo was taken on a 1955 trip she took to Miami to see her brother, Buster, who she actually ended up missing by a day because he'd left for NYC. She and her sister-in-law, Tamassa, who'd traveled all the way there with her, decided to stay and make the most of their vacation. And so it was while they sat poolside at the hotel that they met members of B. B. King's band, who were there on tour. That's who she's pictured with, the bandmates who quickly befriended Marie and Tamassa. The group got along great, and before long both women were off to Havana, Cuba, with the band on a brief visit to the island. And while Marie had lots of stories like this about traveling, sometimes we didn't hear every detail about every story.

Marie was an avid photographer—there are volumes of pictures of family events and vacations. Aside from that infamous

My grandparents—Buddy and Marie—walk with my dad (Wayne, middle) and aunt (Debbie, far left) on a classic stroll on the Atlantic City, NJ, boardwalk. Photo courtesy of the Johnson family archive.

B. B. King encounter, there are photo albums with volumes of pictures she took of family events and vacations, most of them showing how valuable family time, love and connection are. And they're in all these warm, sepia-feeling locations: summertime on front porches and stoops, trips to Atlantic City boardwalks and the beach, visits at relatives' houses all around the area. Lots of pictures of us grandkids balanced on Pop-Pop's lap, or me, my sister and our cousin bundled together like a tiny, Black bouquet of kids, all teeth and grinning eyes. And there's still the occasional picture of her personal trips with girlfriends sprinkled in there. Marie out in the world, Marie having adventures on her own time.

As they got older, Marie and Ms. Marion kept traveling in the form of bus trips to AC and to outlet shopping malls in the surrounding area well into their seventies. Before those years came, Nana Johnson spent a lifetime taking pictures and collecting them in frames, photo albums and boxes. Some of those pictures include the trips they took, fastened behind a cellophane sheet to protect them over time. And while Nana was always smiling, her smiles feel different in those photos—this is a Black woman having her way with the world. This is a Black woman outside. This is a Black woman not cooking and cleaning. This is a Black woman on vacation. For someone who always played the lotto, Nana's travel pictures always looked like she'd won the lottery.

AC was a natural draw for Black people—95 percent of the town's casino-building workforce was Black—and traveling in groups like this was important and practical for Black folks, especially Black women, who'd only just emerged from the dangerous and sexually violent era from the '30s to the '60s that sometimes made it unsafe for them to travel solo. My nanas were part of that generation, a generation of Black women who lived in a time when everyone was hell-bent against their bodily freedom. I'm sure some part of them calculated the safety against the fun of going to AC like this with their girlfriends and friends. Even something like an AC bus trip in the '80s was its own act of continued resistance to a good number of things, primarily the societal belief upheld in households, relationships and public discourses that women, but particularly Black women, are not entitled to joy. Even this micro act of unburdening themselves from their typical roles and responsibilities modeled for the rest of us that taking time away, taking care of yourself, not being beholden to the everyday minutiae of everyone else's needs was not only possible but necessary.

The belief that we are entitled to joy and leisure, especially when it feels as though there's nothing but hardness and struggle in front of us every day, is a gift that many of us need to continually receive. Even now, when I talk to my cousin or my sister or other family members, I hear all their worry that we're not giving enough, doing enough, accomplishing enough despite our different life situations. I see and hear us denying ourselves joy, even small joys. I see the anxieties of failing ourselves and the people around us all the time, and I worry that we're not taking the lessons from Nana Johnson, Nana Murphy, our Pop-Pops and uncle and, dialing even further back, James Eason.

At times I think we've walked away from our familial blueprints even though they contain so much knowledge and perspective. Eason reminds us that it's important to lean into our sense of purpose, our passion for our people and for big things in life and the world around us. I know that his beliefs cost him his life, but that doesn't mean he wasn't doing something right or worthwhile. The fear of consequence will always be there when it comes to wanting to stand up and stand out about the things that matter. This isn't about martyrdom but about purpose. I want us—the generation before me, my generation and the one after me—to remember that it's never too late to live a purposeful life.

Or to know what it would look like to build things together. The Murphy men's dream of Murphy's Bar and Lounge wasn't something commonplace in our family history up until then. Big Mommy's Pop-Pop left the South under family whispers of duress; something bad happened between him and the white people down in small-town Georgia. He came north to build nothing more than a safe, steady, reliable life, and when he sent for his wife and the kids, it was to share the safe life he'd managed to cobble together in New Jersey. Putting that bar together with his sons against the backdrop of a caustic Trenton was no small feat—they had to survive a murderer's row of city poverty; discrimination; pressure from Trenton's Italian, Polish and Irish communities; the local Trenton mob; and the wave of destruction from the MLK riots that changed Trenton forever. Their story of opening the bar is a story of family, togetherness, vision and perseverance.

By 2016 the only grandparent left was Alice Murphy, who, in 2022, sold the family house in Ewing where she lived with Pop-Pop for a good fifty years or so. While Eason was a distant, unknown memory, Big Mommy's Pop-Pop, Pop-Pop, Nana Johnson and Uncle Johnny were fixtures in our lives. I remember so much about each one of them—how Big Mommy's Pop-Pop would sit in a big black leather recliner about eight feet from his TV set and chat with me about *The Andy Griffith Show* or *Perry Mason* while we watched them on days I stayed home from school sick.

Pop-Pop would take my sister and me to Uncle Johnny's house, and sometimes Uncle Johnny would come over and lean into Pop-Pop's driver's side window and they'd talk about working on their houses and how people in the family were doing. Uncle Johnny would always have this really hardworking, kinda sweaty look to him, like he'd been constantly hand mowing the large lawn area that wrapped around his house. In the car, I'd lean forward and look at them talking to each other, or when Pop-Pop would get out of his Town Car and walk around with Uncle Johnny, I'd watch them both saunter around the outside of the house, pointing at a window, or a door, or the landscape.

In college, Nana Johnson and I would spend a good hour or so on the phone—something that confused some of my roommates and friends who'd hear me laughing loud and hard, thinking I was talking to some friend or a girl. We'd chat and gossip about what was going on in both our lives; she loved to gossip about people in the family and tell me stories about Dad growing up. She'd cuss and be curt, smart-mouthed and tender. Her jokes were as dry and sharp as a stick. She'd tell me stories about her and Ms. Marion going on those trips I talked about—to outlet shopping malls, AC or sometimes farther out. She'd ask, "Do you need anything for school?" and even though I usually said no, there'd appear in my campus mailbox a "Thinking of You," "Best Grandson" or "Happy Birthday" card with five to fifteen dollars in it, always with a message written with large handwriting in black marker or ink.

Pop-Pop was my favorite human. Even now, I can picture him strolling down the AC boardwalk when he'd take us there on his days off. In the family, we'd say he had wooden legs because of how stiff and upright he'd walk along the boardwalk, his jaw furiously working itself like a piston as he chewed Doublemint gum. Pop-Pop hummed constantly, drove everywhere in Jersey, loved shopping and—though he wasn't really into gambling—often drove us to AC, where he'd give us a handful of quarters to play in the arcade and then walk with Alice to the casinos and watch her play or wander the boardwalk by himself.

Around 2013 he suffered a stroke that eventually put him out of the house. For several months he lived in care facilities and hospitals, and whenever the troupe of us visited him, I watched his five-foot-ten body with his tree-trunk legs, raspy voice and black, monk-tonsured hair all gradually shrink away. The stroke and the aftermath were fires that seemed to scorch him from the inside—his body wilted, his hair grayed to ash, his hands and feet curled up like burnt newspaper. On his last day we all gathered together at Helene Fuld and spent time saying goodbye one by one. When it was my turn, I walked into his hospital room and looked around, listening to the various machines intermittently beeping. I remember hearing the low hiss of the ventilator, then seeing Pop-Pop in his patient bed. He looked small, and his eyes were as large as soup bowls. When I stood by his bed, his hand was hanging off the edge, and I held it. I remember how dry but soft it felt. We were a mile from where Murphy's Bar and Lounge was. I looked at him for a long time, barely able to talk. A big part of it was that I didn't know how to say goodbye, didn't know what to actually say. I stood there holding his hand and thinking about all the things that I loved doing with him—going to Philly auto shows, watching *All My Children* and *The Price Is Right*, talking to him on the phone about "Bouncy" (his name for Beyoncé), lunches and dinners at Jersey diners all around the state.

But then I started thinking about how aspects of my life by then had included performing for other people, how I wondered if I'd made him proud with what I had and hadn't done up to then. I started thinking about how my own history was gradually piling up—what stories was I making for our family? What were the big and small legacies I was or wasn't leaving behind at this point? I thought about what Pop-Pop's legacy was for me—a mixture of his hard-hat approach to going to work every day, spoiling the women and grandkids in the family with gifts, how he'd play a cassette of Michael Jackson's "Will You Be There" on repeat in the car.

I didn't know what to say then, but I got so scared and sad imagining what we'd be like once he was gone. I started thinking about what it would mean that we'd now stop hearing stories from him and become storytellers about him. Almost immediately, I started worrying that talking about him—at least with real depth and emotion—would be off-limits. I knew that some things were going to be true forever; I wouldn't hear the popping sound of him making bacon in the kitchen or have to set aside time to hear the latest Tiger Woods news. I wouldn't hear "young man" in his warm, raspy voice, and we wouldn't all laugh and repeat some joke he'd just said sitting in his recliner in the living room. And because I knew our family, I knew how hard it was going to be to say to each other the softer, basic things like "I miss him" or "It hurts that he's gone." I also didn't know what, if anything, it meant for me as a quasi-next-in-line man of the family; it felt like whatever blueprint he might've had for that role, we'd never talked about it, and I didn't know where to look for it. Maybe it was in the glove compartment of his Lincoln, or maybe he'd left it years ago in his office desk at Reedman's when he retired. The scarier thought was that maybe it was just in him and wasn't in me. If that was the case, he never got to share it with me before he left.

In June 2001 Nana, Pop-Pop, my mom and my sister escorted me to Philadelphia International Airport to see me off to Houston, where I'd start my first job as a high school English teacher through Teach for America. I remember a lot of random things about that day; for starters, the fact that my family could walk me to the gate because 9/11 wouldn't happen for another three months. The weather was bright and sunny, and the entire airport seemed so lit it felt like we were outside. On the way to my gate, I remember talking to George Clinton, who was sitting by himself outside one of the gates waiting for his flight.

But what I remember the most was us all nervously waiting for my boarding call, each of us looking around, smiling thinly and quickly running out of things to say to pass the final moments. When it was my time, I hugged and kissed everyone goodbye, and when it came down to me and Pop-Pop, I remember his voice breaking slightly. Instead of shaking my hand like he normally would, he pulled me in for a hug and said, "OK, now . . . OK now, young man . . . you be good out there." He let go of me with just the smallest bit of wet in his eyes.

In the hospital that final night, as I held his hand, I leaned over the bed and kissed his face, feeling the whiskers on his cheek like cactus needles. I closed my eyes for a moment because I felt too scared to cry in front of Pop-Pop, but I finally opened my eyes and my mouth to tell him one last story.

PART II

CHAPTER 4

The 5th Dimension

Celebration in America's Face

Young street performer, Odunde Festival, Philadelphia. Photo courtesy of Tre Johnson.

Here, in this here place, we flesh; flesh that weeps, laughs; flesh that dances on bare feet in grass. Love it. Love it hard.
—Baby Suggs, in *Beloved*, Toni Morrison

While my family taught me how to make stories and memories out of places, the wider Black community has continually reminded me we have the ability to make a celebration out of anything. That's been one of our best community powers—culturally terraforming some of the most unlikely spaces into a shield, a protective Black barrier. As Black folks, we use the city, nature, music and more to create spaces that allow us to breathe.

Our artists have always known this. Baldwin once wrote about how being in the US was choking him. "I needed to be in a place," he wrote, "where I could breathe and not feel someone's hand on my throat." That was 1977; in 2022 musician Moses Sumney released *Blackalachia*, an hour-long mixed-medium project that he stated came from the feeling that he "needed a space to articulate my own loneliness, not at the level of state, or nation, or race or place."

The heavier gentrification waves in major US cities—Philly, DC, Chicago, LA, Detroit, Atlanta—have made it both harder and more necessary for us to come up with the means to create spaces for ourselves. Local restaurants and establishments have gradually adopted implicitly racist dress codes banning entry for customers wearing ball caps, sneakers, athletic wear and sports jerseys, and schools, recreation centers and libraries have been closed down. In Philly, the Five Spot and Fluid Nightclub, popular hip-hop and DJ spots that boasted customers could brush shoulders with artists like the Roots, Bilal and Jill Scott while dancing and drinking, were both gone by the 2010s. More than just dance spots, these places were cultural hubs, joints where you'd connect with people, particularly Black people. The first time I went to Fluid, located on a little side street right off deep South Street in Philly, was with some hip-hop heads who I'd become friends with not long after I moved there in 2006. It was a Saturday night, and the place was not just packed but packed with Black folks I knew—educators, activists, restaurant folks, theater people—and everyone was crammed in this tiny space, bodies glued to each other. That night Questlove was DJing, and I was amazed that I lived in a city where I could step out at night and party with a Black star like that.

But before long, gentrification hit Philly. As white people and richer people moved back, policies, police and boundaries started changing fast. We were losing third places and cultural spaces fast as downtowns developed new spaces for new people, and we were further culturally pushed out of city centers. Cities started feeling hostile; new restaurants and their hipster, preppy or progressive clientele turned their noses up at us. Police patterns increased in downtown areas, and social policing patterns started matching them. Despite the surge of Black pride and visibility that came with Obama's win in 2008, something parallel was happening, too; that same period seemed to mark a time of cultural changes in a lot of culturally Black cities. Those places were starting to feel like a closed fist crushing and squeezing us out of the picture.

But we've also found ways to pry those hands back open with our genius ability to reclaim a mixture of joy and community in the city through the streets. No one's doing this better than Philadelphia, where our mix of festivals, fun and fast riding displays a multitude of traditions that we use to be in celebration with each other. And nothing showcases our collective and individual genius ability to celebrate more than Philly's Black Summer.

A few years into its existence, Lois Fernandez said this about the Odunde festival: "We didn't have anything to connect to. The whites have the Mummers, Now we have ODUNDE."

My family might've been light on traditions, but the ones we had stuck hard. When summer came around, my parents loaded us up and drove south on I-95 into South Philly to go to Odunde, the Black diaspora festival stretching several blocks that runs each June. Odunde started in 1975 thanks to Lois Fernandez and is considered to be the largest Black street festival in the country. And while there's year-round cultural programming in schools and communities around Philly, the crown event is the June weekend festival where Black folks from all over the tri-state area stroll the transformed promenade.

For as long as I've been going to Odunde, it's always blazing hot and packed shoulder to shoulder with Black people. Everyone's making their way along Odunde's main drag on South Street, where the festival starts around South Fifteenth Street and stretches about a mile, splintering onto a series of side streets. Odunde turns South Philly into a Black bazaar; all along the corridor a series of Black-owned kiosks sell everything from self-published books to homemade incense and perfumes, to pro-Black slogan T-shirts with phrases like "I AM A KING" or "Black History Is All History," to anything under the sun made with a kente pattern. And pamphlets, so many pamphlets, all the pamphlets—inviting people to join local movements or temples, offering free legal advice, providing FYIs about new after-school or daycare programs, or warning about the city's latest effort to close a school or church.

The pavement bakes like it's being slow cooked by an underground grill. Black folks cool themselves off under the shade of rowhomes, sitting peacefully on stoops sharing Styrofoam containers of soul food—brown-topped mac 'n' cheese, collard greens swimming in their juices, moist-meat fried chicken with flaky skin, sweet potatoes basking in little lakes of butter. Brothers blotting their faces with damp washcloths and sweaty sleeveless undershirts sell bottled water out of coolers for a dollar. Somehow, music seems to come from everywhere—trees, vendors, off the flavored water ice, through the African beads and jewelry, from the Black street performers doing acrobatic routines shirtless or in Power Rangers or Spider-Man costumes. They balance on one hand, and there's music in the crowd's reaction, as well as through the small, tinny speakers they bring for their performances.

It's also common to constantly run into people you know the whole time—this happened to my parents when they'd take us back in the '80s, and now, having lived in Philly for almost twenty years, it happens to me. Over the years, I've run into friends, cousins, coworkers, Uber drivers, former students, faces that I see around town. Odunde's a big Black church, and even if you've just seen someone yesterday, running into each other at Odunde always feels different. You'll see people stop, hug, talk, take a pic together and keep it moving. Five minutes later, you'll probably do the same thing with someone else.

Everything's picturesque at Odunde: the Black cowboys strutting down South Philly blocks, a soundstage with throwback R&B acts, the long bins of food, Black people fanning themselves, Black folks holding clothes up against their bodies to measure them, open-door house parties right off South Street, where Black folks mill on tiny city lawns.

But some of the most entertaining views come from the

proud Black Afrocentric art for sale at the festival. A lot of these pieces mix religious themes with anachronistic cultural references that sometimes ends up being pretty fucking hilarious to look at, like the painting of Malcolm X dropping MLK a behind-the-back, no-look pass as they run a two-on-two fast break in their black dress suits against two white police officers who can only watch the play unfold in awe in a sold-out basketball arena. Others are sometimes RIP-tributes: a scene featuring Aaliyah, DMX, Kobe (awkwardly decked out in Lakers gear), Nipsey Hussle, Chadwick Boseman (in Black Panther costume) and Tupac enjoying drinks in a dark-lit room with the word "Forever" written on the wall behind them. Another homage painting also features Kobe, and fallen rappers Tupac and Nipsey; the three men are decked out in safari gear, riding horses in front of a waterfall on an expedition.

I love their absurdity. I love their earnestness. I love that they love us. I imagine them hanging in TV rooms, church halls, and mom-and-pop restaurants. I love knowing that as much as I admire the effort someone put into making these art pieces, I'd never hang one of these up in my life.

I have no idea where I'd hang a painting with Maya Angelou, Grace Jones, Kamala Harris and Megan Thee Stallion playing double Dutch—but I get it.

But this all is why I and so many Black people love Odunde: this beautiful explosion of Black pride, history, food and culture that blows in and out of Philly on a June weekend with a Black boom and disappears in a flash.

> *You know the kids gon' act a fool*
> *When you stop the programs for after school*
> —Kanye West, "We Don't Care"

When I moved to Philly back in 2006, the flash mob phenomenon was kicking off. Groups of young Black kids, mostly teens, hopped up on the blended energy of *Naruto*, *Dragon Ball Z* and a rapidly disappearing downtown, would race around Center City causing beautiful chaos. These flashes were genius, just scores of kids going Super Saiyan in these streets, transforming themselves and each other into pure forms of excitement. They'd always take me by complete surprise; I'd be walking down Walnut or South Street headed to a shop and then—wham!—I swore it was like these kids materialized out of the concrete, fire hydrants, shop windows, street poles.

These flash mobs were flawlessly executed, coordinated in school and through texts, social media and word of mouth. I usually found myself caught up in one walking to the Whole Foods on South Street; all of a sudden there'd be a swarm of laughing, dancing, Nike- and tight-jeans-wearing kids flooding the block like a street production of *West Side Story*. The flash mobs always played out the same way—everyone would gather at an intersection where a couple kids would be playing music over their cell phone or through some Five Below portable speaker, and they'd all dance around the rest of us walking by, hugging each other or spinning in small groups.

These kids were the beginning of a new multihyphenate, polyglot generation making new connections between music, art, gender, language, technology and space. They created new language through YouTube comments, IG and Facebook posts and DMs, and text chains, and fused bits of pop-culture inspiration ranging from *SpongeBob* to Soulja Boy to connect and have fun.

By the '00s to the early '10s, everything else was being taken away from them in Philly. The Gallery and Liberty Place downtown malls placed curfews on minors, arcades and skating rinks were nowhere to be found, and recent budget moves by Black Philly mayor Michael Nutter had resulted in libraries in a lot of Black communities closing down. There was really nowhere for kids to take all themselves to hang, burn off energy and be out the house, and nobody was making space for them anymore.

They were routinely being chased out of pizza joints and Center City shops, followed and reported on the subway. And these were kids already running out of their schools, and who could blame them—I'd visited places like William Penn High School and charter schools around the city, and a lot of them felt like dank prisons. William Penn was actually shut down and condemned by the district and the city, but only after students had attended a school with boarded-up windows, dank dangerous hallways and little natural light for years.

At one point, a new district-wide reimagining of schools allowed operators to essentially cordon off parts of the buildings and partner with places like Camelot Education, who turned the upper floors into highly regimented, restrictive environments for kids deemed to be problem students. You spend six or seven hours every day in a place like that, and yeah, you might be inspired to try some new shit, too.

So what these kids did through the flash mob scene is nothing short of genius; they turned to DIY modes to create whole new hangout hubs online that they manifested on the streets.

What choice did they have?

Problem was, at that same time Mayor Nutter and gentrification were both happening to Black Philadelphia. In Nutter's eyes, the flash mob scene was about Black kids, as he said in an interview, "running amok." In his version of a "Pound Cake" speech, Mayor Nutter said to his church congregation that these Black kids "damaged your own race."

Other local figures followed his lead, too. Councilman Jim Kenney called flash mobs acts of "urban terrorism," and soon authorities like the Philly police and the FBI were trying to monitor and decipher conversations over social media comments sections, trying to get the jump on these kids. As someone who came in promising to be friendly to Center City downtown businesses and residents by cleaning that area up, Nutter continued to crack down hard on the phenomenon; he instituted a night curfew requiring minors to be off the streets by 9 p.m. unless they were accompanied by an adult.

By 2012, between police surveillance, fines of $300 imposed on parents and guardians for their kids' involvement and threats to deactivate evening use of student public transit passes, the Philly flash mob scene came to an end. And all that while the world was rapidly changing; by the time Trump came around it'd already felt like places like Philly were on a drive to make their cities "great" again. I think a lot of us were in a bit of a cultural shock; we were left wondering how it all could have changed so fast. Time didn't only march on, it felt like it marched on us, too.

And so with the world trying to leave us behind, we found a way to catch up and not be forgotten.

✧ ✧ ✧

If you stand around long enough, you start to think it's a parade, especially the first couple of times seeing their procession. They feel like they're coming from another dimension, this series of Black Mad Maxes on their steeds. They're loud, loud-loud, but their riding is truly lightning-quick artistry. I've seen these troupes every season except winter for years, and Philly, despite its self-professed, self-congratulatory "progressive" label, hates these brothers riding around like this.

No one tells you how to feel about them when they rip down the street, but my favorite thing is to close my eyes for a moment and feel it in my body. That deep, rumbling buzz of their engines, that constant din of a troupe of them zipping down Broad Street or leaning hard as they race around the oval outside of the Philadelphia Art Museum. No one tells you what you're supposed to do about them when you see them, neither—should you be yelling at them to stop? Should you be cheering them on? Let's cheer them on, mostly. And I know that's complicated—these are Black folks on Honda and Kawasaki ATVs, dirt bikes and tri bikes—and I also know that, for whatever reason, more and more of these riders have strayed from the old showboating promenade.

On Philly summer nights, dozens of these riders would take to South Street and slow down traffic and pedestrian rubber-neckers as the same collection of ATVs, tri bikes and decked-out cars with wild-ass racing lights and bright colors peacocked their way down the block, music pounding from their speakers. Those Black folks were celebrating summer, celebrating payday, celebrating being able to take your love out on a ride, celebrating eating and music and Philly summer heat. Those moments are seen as nuisances just as much as the non-summer joyriding, where folks now have spiraled off South Street and spread to hot spots around the city.

During the Philly summers, you can routinely see groups of bikers gathered at neighborhood gas stations before they head down Broad and South Streets to flex for people. Photo courtesy of Tre Johnson.

To some degree, joy like this can't be contained. And when they go fast, man, they go so fast! Brothers standing up on their rides and feeling the wind whip their T-shirts against their bodies. Their arms locked tight on the grips, their bodies pulled taut when they go 12 o'clock on their wheels. I mean, this is a thing to see and behold. These Black riders stand so upright on their bikes, their shadows look like they're falling off the back seats.

Like the flash mobs, it's hard to tell whether there's actual music around them or you're imagining the music in your head. I see them riding, reaching out and dapping each other as their girls grasp their shirts and jackets, sometimes burying their faces into the rider's back or leaning back and nodding and playfully shit talking each other.

But I love it all, the freestyling, the freedom, the artistry of stunting, the put-on casualness of gliding through parts of the city with no care, no stress and sometimes no helmets.

They move in packs of eight, ten, fifteen or thirty, and you'll catch them laughing at each other, giving directions about where to turn and go next, tossing a look over at the rest of us idiots complying with just boring-ass walking through Center City, downtown Wherever.

For a lot of people, this behavior is flagrant, "loud," dangerous and uncivilized. They liken it to crime without warranting why, and often it seems the biggest crime is the affront to their comfort and convenience.

When you dare to stunt around town it comes with the territory that you'll create some havoc—whole traffic lanes, lights and pedestrians are made to slow to a crawl or standstill when you come through. But this is a good thing in my eyes, a beautiful thing; you're made to watch how these riders have cracked the code of their city living.

There's a code to Black gatherings, too. This comes to mind

whenever I've gone to Philly's Roots Picnic—the other Black Summer tradition—for the last several years. The Roots Picnic has been around since 2008. It started off in smaller spots like Penn's Landing before gaining more attention through a combination of inviting big cultural acts and word of mouth. By 2017 the outdoor music festival had moved to a slightly larger space at Philadelphia's waterfront along Columbus Boulevard, taking over a wide-open ground that looks out over the Delaware into Camden, New Jersey. And each time, the swell of attendees, particularly Black folks, grew and grew, stretching beyond the festival grounds.

And the whole time, the Legendary Roots Crew essentially curated a live music playlist of mainly Black artists to perform. The festival put the diaspora on full display. Over the years the spectrum of acts has run from John Legend to Naughty by Nature, Clipse to Gary Clark Jr., Snoop Dogg to Willow Smith. The Roots often play with the biggest headliners as the backing band, too, performing with Mary J. Blige, Pharrell and Erykah Badu. The vibe of the Roots Picnic reflects this spread, capturing the array of Black folks living in the Philly area, who could each find their niche at the picnic.

The Roots Picnic has continued to be a place of Black discovery. Something stirs in my body when I imbibe a Black artist that I didn't know or thought I knew. It's a stage to listen to and understand each other better—Black artist to Black fan—with an invisible chord piping love back and forth between us. Roots tends to feel like a healing place, too.

Take what happens at events like Philly's annual Roots Picnic. At the 2017 Roots Picnic, I stood in a crowd listening to *A Seat at the Table*–era Solange on a small stage. *A Seat* is a continuous anthem to Black business ownership, beauty, and Blackness itself.

So on that summer night in Philly I stared through the throng, and everyone looked luminescent in the glow of the stage lights, their skin shimmering from the combination of Philly humidity and summer sheen.

I watched a circle of Black women in musical, emotional, spiritual rapture. I saw one sister rest her elbow on the shoulder of another, both of their eyes shut as they mouthed the words along with Knowles. In another spot along this informal circle, three Black women faced each other, two with their backs to the stage. They were slightly hunched over, legs spaced to steady themselves on the slightly muddy concert ground, and as they looked at each other, they sang into each other's faces in their circle.

Rapturous.

That's what the performance felt like; the energy that Solange vibrated cascaded off the stage and housed itself in Black people all around the crowd. Black couples of all hues, genders and sexualities leaned on each other. I watched one woman ceremoniously unbundle her hair and let it drop onto her bare shoulders.

At one point, Solange descended into the crowd and was carried across the wave of Black hands. There was enthusiasm but also a respectful parting and adoration for her as she made her way through everyone. A light followed her as she moved in a peaceful, harmonic procession.

✿ ✿ ✿

> *'Cause I'm close—to the streets*
> *To the beach, the bitches, the niggas*
> —Mos Def, "Close Edge"

All hail the genius of the Philly Black Summer! A two-month stretch of art and ATVs, open-air festivals and the awesome June transformation of South Street into a Black promenade! Hot bodies bursting with sweat bump and bounce because every block is bustling with Black folks. To be Black here in the summer is to fall in love with Philadelphia all over again. It's to be rejuvenated through the month-to-month magic of mashing our bodies together in festival food lines, making our mouths move to the music at Roots Picnic, motioning from front stoops to get over here, elbows out on open car windows hollering and nodding at folks, brow wiping with washcloths and grilling in the park.

Philly's Black Summer is about being together.

About trying to be at every possible event and function to see people.

About looking cute.

About wringing every bit of the summer out of every day by hanging out and doing as many things as possible together.

Philly's Black Summer has become the antidote to the physical and cultural erosion that has taken place over the last ten to twelve years. "We outside" has now become an update about how we're moving and claiming spaces, and in Philly, that means that summertime has the feel of a throwback to when the city was still seen as a Black city. Summer feels like the time when the best Black stories happen in the city, and that's why August's BlackStar Film Festival is the perfect example of celebrating the range of "we" in Philly.

Why is Maori Karmael Holmes's BlackStar Film Festival genius? Because for over a decade, Black Star Film Festival has been a three-to-four-day event that transforms Philly's cultural spaces into an ephemeral Chocolate City. It's a constant celebration the whole time; film screenings can be entirely emotional experiences. People cheer as friends and fans when names they know and love appear on the title screens or in the credits, and the feelings don't stop there. The Black woman who sat behind me at the screening of Staceyann Chin's documentary *A Mother Apart* quietly talked back to the film several times. People come here and celebrate these movies with their whole heart, you know? And more importantly, we're all allowed to do that at the festival. It feels like being in Paris seeing *Black Panther* all over again, or the times I saw *Creed* or *Get Out* down at Philly's old Riverview theater down along Columbus Boulevard, how we'd all erupt in unison. So if you haven't been to BlackStar, I want you to imagine all your favorite times seeing a movie with an all-Black audience and multiply it by days.

BlackStar's got the biggest range of Black films whose subject matter spans grief, sexuality, love, family and legacy. It's a genius curation of stories; I've seen Black absurdism, comedy, romance and sci-fi—sometimes in the same film. The festival experience is a Black fun house that's part reflection, part imagination, and whether I'm watching the films or the people, I always end up getting swept up in how much energy there is when we're all together. There, I see all these more imaginative, wider versions of myself—who or what else I could be, what stories I tell myself or don't about my past, my pain, my dreams, my heart. BlackStar is a journal.

I think a lot of us go there and are dazzled; Black folks are also stepping out there in their flyest, finest outfits. You see this beautiful jumble of jumpers and jumpsuits, clever thrift-store style ensembles, dresses, kicks that I've never seen before. Just style on style, looks on looks. Sometimes I missed screenings or was way late because I was so stressed laying out and trying on outfits, wanting to show up and show out in style. The festival's opening and closing night parties will leave you with a deep, quiet, secret shame for not looking fly. BlackStar is a fashion show.

Everyone looks like a star; everyone feels like a star. You're photographed by other festivalgoers or event staff or press. You just feel beautiful there, and you're taken by how beautiful everyone around you looks and feels. Someone might stop you to tell you how good you look and then keep it moving with nothing more than that compliment. BlackStar is a crush.

Maori created the kind of space not only where every type of Black person can find a niche but also, if you're willing to open your eyes and your heart, you can see all the notches that Black people can fit in and jump from. It can be literally hard to step back out into the real world where there's nothing that feels like this.

BlackStar is one of the essential places for us to gather as a community. And when we're together in a community setting, it's only natural that we want to share and tell each other stories. BlackStar taps into that, on- and off-screen—everyone's milling about sharing stories either because they're catching up with each other or talking about one of the short films, documentaries or feature-length films they've just seen. It can feel so special; you see people come out of viewing rooms and into the festival space, eyes wet with feelings, soapy with so much to say about what they just saw, just experienced, and wham—you're back in a throng of us Black folks, all jittering with this energy of having just seen a new Black light shone through someone's story.

And as these stories light up connections inside of you, you start seeing all these ways about how we can be simultaneously unique and connected through our stories. That you can see new vistas and still feel at home. That you can be in a galaxy of stories and stand there and point to the stars you know and still have the heart space to discover new ones. Sometimes I have been giddy to learn something new about myself that I hadn't realized until I saw a particular film or short.

I have been pensive when a story has made me remember that there are parts of myself that I've forgotten.

There are moments and scenes inside some projects that make me pause and hold my breath. I've walked out of viewings, reached for my phone and texted an acquaintance that I hadn't thought of in a while and suddenly missed and wanted to connect with again. I have walked out suddenly having the language and the love to share words with someone that I'd locked away or finally realized about myself, them or us together.

BlackStar is a constellation.

As a matter of fact, I don't want to go back to the real world after being in BlackStar's Chocolate City.

The world is still set up for us to navigate and celebrate Blackness through a series of red lights and green lights, and those permissions and denials are the reasons we need to consider about why we sometimes do things like become flash mobs and urban ATV roadies. There is an inability in society at large to give space to all the ways that we want to be able to express ourselves, love ourselves, hear ourselves, celebrate ourselves and understand the types of freedoms we want. We deserve not only canvases to be contradictory but also ones to be creative and free. The standards of when and how we can do so are part of what drives us to be out in these streets. Add to that how often non-Black people disparage us, along with the pressure that so many of us feel to artificially prop ourselves up for others' comfort or perceptions, and well, yes, I find myself wanting to flash mob on Tuesday and slide my ass onto a dirt bike come the weekend, too.

If we restrict people's movements and dreams, the only result is a nightmare society of socially and politically policing each other. That we endure all of this as Black people and still do not resort to the litany of actions that others do for often even smaller slights, is cause for celebration.

Music, festivals and reunions transport our emotional selves to other planes, where we traverse and transcend time. I've never been on an ATV or dirt bike, have never rushed into the middle of downtown to join a throng of Black teens in a flash mob. But I've done my own things; I've stood in that ice-cold line to see *Black Panther* and swooned in a crowd of us as we sang along with Solange at the Roots Picnic.

I've taken retreats with other Black folks and by myself, standing on beaches and wandering woods going deep on each other and on myself. I've stood naked in cabins deep in Napa and let life return me to myself. Those were the times that I felt like Moses Sumney; I'd taken myself out of a restrictive space and let myself spiritually and creatively breathe. I stopped worrying about the usual shit—bills, racism, police, more bills, the cloudiness that can come with creativity and capitalism—and felt pores in every part of my body and mind open up and sigh. Those were times that the idea of retreats, and retreating from society, felt like peeking into another dimension of happiness, one where so much more felt possible.

I want Black people to have air, more air for us to celebrate and be celebrated by each other. I want us to rush to any and all open spaces and claim them with our joy, to lean into the lands around us and lean against trees, lie in grass, kiss in lakes. I started listening to the 5th Dimension after seeing them in the Questlove documentary *Summer of Soul*, mainly drawn by the group's ability to harness the energy of open spaces, love and music to create more music. The 5th Dimension toured the country bringing their beautiful, uplifting, lyrical, literal, harmonious escape sounds to us, appearing like something between nymphs and new-age church emissaries. Their music plays with the notions of time, boundaries and reality, pushing Black people to remember that there was, is and forever will be more to this life than just the many things that make it feel impossible. Their song "Skinny Man" was written in awe of a man who leads an independent life outside society, sustaining himself on the land. The skinny man lives on a hill in a house with a "roof top thatched," and he's free, uninhibited, unbound, able to explore himself without worrying about "school or work[ing] like a fool."

The 5th Dimension's view was one of love, enlightenment and a joy for living. This included the idea that we've got time; time to live, to love, to try living and loving. Besides "Skinny Man," their album *The Age of Aquarius* is full of songs about a second chance at life. "Don'tcha Hear Me Callin' to Ya" and the album's opener, "Aquarius/Let the Sunshine In (Flesh Failures)," say that right here, right now, there's a possibility of transformation in our lives and that the might of love, and of celebrating love and life, are some of the biggest antidotes to oppression. "You gotta get away from it all and let it all hang out," they harmonize in "The Hideaway."

The fifth dimension is the space that Black people occupy when we're together. The other dimensions, even the third, somehow seem to render us flat still, smoothing out narratives and nuances about Black lives into manageable, controllable nubs. When we're together in this dimension, the fifth, I think there's a resurgence of belief that anything's possible, particularly when we reach out to each other to build a better collective community. The act of celebration in the affinity of all-Black abstract or concrete spaces is essential to this; these spaces open up mini portals inside of each one of us that, when nurtured, encourage us to think more widely about what our interior and exterior lives have to offer.

It is important for Black people to seek out and move through modes of celebration of all types. I am continually reminded to "mark my moments," to not thoughtlessly move on from life's gifts as they happen. To pause, acknowledge and be in community with people—Black people in particular—in the expanse of joy, life and freedom that comes with being together.

Which is to say that I've known the tensions of needing to celebrate and get away from things not just as a form of resistance but also as a celebration of reminding myself how lucky I am to be alive, how beautiful to be Black and alive.

To be Black and alive and in community with myself and my people. I know what it means to embrace celebration as a way to push the bounds of what we've been told is allowable, to rejuvenate ourselves and love on each other knowing how often it might also rankle or inspire envy in others.

I know that Black folks in purposeful communities are the biggest flame, sometimes seen as potentially destructive and other times as irresistibly magnetic. Together, our love and community are magnetic because together we are the skinny man, a truth that there are other dimensions to this existence that don't require permission.

CHAPTER 5

What Doesn't Kill You Only Mutates and Tries Again

Performance in the Streets

Q-Tip from A Tribe Called Quest performs at an NYC festival back in 2017, right after the group reunited and released We Got It from Here.
Photo courtesy of Tre Johnson.

It's a combination of . . . wrestling with myself to be honest,
with me. If I'm honest with me, I've got to be honest with the
audience.

—Dick Gregory, 1966 KVOS interview

just found out that Dick Gregory died." We were all seated
in Radio City Music Hall enjoying a night of Chappelle and
Friends, the previously reclusive comedian's return to the
performance stage. That night we had been treated to several
cameo performances by artists like Hannibal Buress and a
pre–"This Is America" Childish Gambino. This was a big deal at
the time; it was 2017 and Chappelle was only relatively "back"
after performing one of the most talked-about disappearing acts
in history when he left behind $50 million and the uber-popular
Chappelle's Show. That summer night NYC came out to see this
comic messiah-turned-pariah; as people headed to their seats, I
saw Justin Timberlake and Jessica Biel. Robin Roberts strode
down the aisle. And while the preceding acts were overall great,
there was a palpable buzz as everyone waited for Chappelle to
take the stage. But it was only during the encore that he came
back on looking suddenly forlorn and beaten after what seemed
to be a hit set with the audience.

The news that Dick Gregory had died during the course of

those performances sent a chill through the theater for those of us who knew who he was.

Out on the street outside the venue, we milled about, a few of us strangers talking to each other about both the show and the news. There was some shock; death was a cold breeze on a sticky August summer night. I think a lot of things were on our minds at that moment. For one thing, Gregory probably felt so old to us by then that it seemed like he'd beaten death; over the course of his twenty-first-century appearances, it was becoming clear that he was in a slow mental decline. But it was also clear in our minds how much Gregory's boldness as a performer was exactly why Buress, Gambino and Chappelle were all able to do the sort of comedy and entertainment they'd become known for.

And while countless people have been doing comedy, both then and now, one of my favorites has been Dick Gregory. After that NYC night, I started going backwards through his life and work, and over the next several years I got to understand the power of his career and legacy.

That night I started thinking about how Black performances create social, cultural and political spaces for us in society. I thought about how in college, my roommate Joel's friend Sterling would always put on a performance to get white boys out of our room. Sterling was short and soft-stocky, built like Winnie-the-Pooh, with sleepy, downturned eyes and this Black DC drawl to his voice. Every time he came by, he had a bottle of lime-yellow Gatorade in his hand and either a white washcloth or hand towel sitting on his shoulder. He was always funny, chill and good for stopping by and telling us stories about growing up in DC. He loved to eat our food in the fridge or bring by some DC go-go mixtape or a used PlayStation game. He always had us laughing; he was raunchy, quick-witted and smart. I don't even know how he met Joel, but soon he was my friend, too, and so whenever he came by when Joel wasn't around, we'd get into whatever, usually music or video games.

But anytime Sterling was over, he had one rule: He didn't want to see any white people. I don't know where it came from. It might've been that, as a DC kid who grew up in the hood, he wasn't used to hanging around white kids, and coming to UMD—where there were so many in every lecture room, dining hall, library and all up in the student union—he felt he needed a break. Like, maybe being around so many white kids his age and most likely having almost no professors who weren't white felt abnormal to him. If I remember right, Sterling graduated from one of the DC public schools that were almost always all-Black back then—high schools like Anacostia, Ballou, Dunbar, where there'd maybe be the occasional white teacher here and there, but you definitely had hardly any white kids in your class. And I imagine that like in a lot of Black neighborhoods, the only other time he ever really ran into white people was when it was a cop car rolling down your block.

Or sidling up alongside you.

And our dorm floor that year was mostly white; Joel and I were definitely the only Black boys. So any time one of the white boys would see our open door and stop in while Sterling was there, he'd slide into this extra version of his DC self. He became all Black DC drawl, sometimes sliding on his durag. He'd start talking slick to whoever was standing in the room, doing things like calling them "bama," or he'd get up in the middle of the conversation with whoever was trying to talk to us and turn up the stereo (our stereo!). He brought the room down to the chilliness of ice with this act, transforming from our loveable, Black Kramer-like character to embody every ignorant and aggressive hood stereotype to make it clear that they weren't welcome when he was around. The white boy would shift from foot to foot, not sure how to hang around, and would always end up leaving. As they left, we'd laugh, and the room would get warm all over again. He only needed to do this a couple of times; after a while, people would start to stop by, see Sterling was in the room and keep on walking.

Sterling knew the value of putting on a performance. It was genius the way he did it; I loved watching him play the part of the thug, a boogeyman that a lot of these college kids were afraid of. These were kids who still only knew Black people through rap and music videos, pro and college teams and the local news. For them, Sterling's DC persona was like something that had leaped off those screens or out of those *Sports Illustrated* issues, something they'd managed to mostly avoid and now here he was, a DC thug, right up in their dorm room.

"Watch this," Sterling would whisper when one of those boys would come by, and then he'd get into character, his own Black method acting, and the show would begin. He's the first example that comes to my mind of how genius Black performances can be, especially when these performances are used to wreak havoc on the atmosphere around us so that we've got space to move. So, even when it sometimes made me uncomfortable, I eventually appreciated Sterling's little act, because it taught me a lot about having a right to my own space, safety and sanity.

I should probably have a picture of him hanging on my wall.

A two-paneled black-and-white mug-shot photo of Dick Gregory I found in an antique shop in Lambertville, New Jersey, hovers over the brown record player cabinet in my second-floor walk-up. One word appears beneath his face in bold, black capital letters: "NEEDED."

It's the campaign poster for the 1968 presidential election when Gregory was a write-in candidate for the Freedom and Peace Party. He and his running mate, white author and activist Mark Lane, received almost fifty thousand votes in the national election.

Gregory's brilliance came from the comedian's ability to

blend humor and politics into a satirical performance that didn't require compartmentalization.

Instead, the coolness that he maintained standing in front of white comedy-club and night-lounge crowds was the same one he used to wade into on-the-ground activities during the Civil Rights Movement. By his own count, by 1968 he'd been arrested nearly fifty times for his civil unrest actions. And it's not like they all went victoriously; his attempts to pacify protestors during the Watts riots resulted in him getting shot in the leg.

I love watching Dick Gregory go to work on stage. I started watching a lot of old clips and interviews through YouTube and documentaries. Take some time to watch some of his stand-up routines. You'll see Gregory's trademark biting, dry honesty that he delivered with a slow-burning cigarette and flat voice. With those deadpan stares and that wry smile, Gregory delivered his quips with the same casual quickness of tapping his cigarette— and let his audiences sit with the joke, the awkward truths he revealed lingering like smoke from the end of a joint.

To me, his performances show how aware he was of the line he was walking—he knew that white racial animosity was such a whimsical, flimsy, ever-present thing that could turn on you with the flick of a punch line.

Gregory was a master at merging politics, performance and personality. In his 1964 autobiography *Nigger*, he talks about navigating the racial and cultural climates that intersected against the backdrop of increased Black mobility and the Civil Rights Movement. Here was a brother who knew and relished the fact that he was tempting fate in the mostly white rooms he found himself in, all while also being tracked, jailed, beaten and harassed by authorities from both the FBI and police in every state he set foot in. He was even on J. Edgar Hoover's watchlist during the height of that 1968 presidential campaign; the FBI head went so far as to try and corral the mafia to use "sophisticated . . . untraceable means of neutralizing Gregory," as revealed in a notorious 1968 memo from Hoover to President Johnson that has now been reproduced in *The Washington Post*, *Chicago Tribune* and other media outlets.

Antiwar, antipoverty, anti-racist and anti-capitalist Gregory leveraged the popularity of his comedy routines to talk in large-room forums and radio interviews and speak to students, faculty members, journalists and public figures about everyday national and global politics. That's part of what irked someone like Hoover so much; he considered Gregory's Black nationalist commentary and criticism of the United States to be a complete threat to the nation's power and control. Gregory was sublime when it came to pointing out how America was so busy playing in Black people's faces without considering how gaslighting us might blow up in their face. Like many social thinkers and activists at the time, Gregory was especially aware of how two-faced America was.

He laid some of this out as a guest at UCLA in 1968, brought there on the heels of his involvement in the Civil Rights Movement and all the horrors he'd seen. He shared several thoughts about the US, race, war and politics. In my favorite stretch of that speech, he talks about the intersection of Black folks, fighting and freedom:

> *You shouldn't have no doubt in your mind that Black folks do love to kill for freedom. Y'all running around talking nonviolence and this and that, but your tax money is taking Black folks in the army and teaching them how to be good killers for freedom . . . and while they do that, you give their mama an allotment check. . . . If you sick enough to believe that when he comes back home he's not going to do the same things to liberate his Black mama, you out of your mind.*

Gregory swore he'd never get into politics because you only "lose your freedom of speech" and felt that "the two-party system is obsolete, so corrupt and immoral, they cannot solve the problems confronting the masses of the people in this country." Because he was more known as a comedian and entertainer, people couldn't figure out if Gregory's run for office was real or really a joke. Some of it felt draped in his brand of performing; like, of course he was "running for office" because by then Gregory was seen as this smartass brother. He'd stood in front of all those white audiences over the years, cigarette keeping him steady, looking like he was waiting for the firing squad. Being at those marches and protests in Alabama, Mississippi, Chicago, gave him the perspective that he needed to fight, on and off the stage. This was a man who started fasting as a form of protest, letting his body wither down to damn near his cellular structure. If Gregory was performing, he was committed to the bit, and he was doing it for the betterment of all of us. I'll take that performance over today's social media activists twenty times over.

By the time Gregory's recorded thoughts on Ferguson and Mike Brown were captured in a 2014 *Time* piece, the activist's mind had devolved into hysteria, consumed by paranoias about government machinations, political killings and our connections to the universe.

In the short video accompanying the article he stands under the street sign for Dick Gregory Place, and the video slides into a series of clips showing Black people clogging the streets and riding down boulevards on top of cars, shirtless Black men cruising and clapping each other's backs in the St. Louis heat. Mike Brown's mother is seen standing with relatives at his murder site; they collectively raise their arms in thanks as a driver honks his horn to show his love and support. "This is emotion," Gregory says as the video rolls footage of Black St. Louisans in various states of anger, exasperation and disbelief. "If it wasn't for television, we Black folks wouldn't have had the Civil Rights stuff, because if people couldn't see it, there's no way you could convince someone."

He never lost the edge of injustice, but his performances seemed to have lost an edge of lucidity as a result of his mental state, beliefs and getting old. It's wild watching footage of him late in life or hearing people talk about working and being around him during those years, how even then he was still performing and pontificating about politics. There was a restlessness about Gregory that suggested that even then he didn't feel like he was doing enough to wake people up or change the ways that we were still being treated in America.

I don't know yet what it's like to see the end of your life coming and have to decide how you spend those last days. Will I choose to be as outspoken, agitated and wry as Gregory was on his way out? What will my mind overflow with? What words will gurgle behind my lips and fight to come out? To what extent will I know how coherent or incoherent I sound to people while I've seen the world's frequencies barely changing after so long? What will I want to leave behind before I go, even in my last days?

In his last days, Gregory tended to sound like the ranting elder at the holiday table. With his Gandalf-like white beard and narrow face, he died chock-full of things left to say about his conspiracies, paranoias and beliefs about how intrinsically sinister the country, the government and so many public leaders were. When he could've chosen to go silently off into the night, Gregory instead risked it all by continuing to talk and shout until the darkness finally came for him.

✩ ✩ ✩

> *I had created this, uh, public persona, this public illusion, and it held me hostage.*
> —Lauryn Hill, "Interlude 1," *MTV Unplugged No. 2.0*

Not quite a rap line, but a bar all the same. And another performer comes to mind who spit these kinds of lines whenever she had the chance to take or claim center stage. Lorraine O'Grady—social worker, counselor, culture writer, artist—strode into NYC art galleries in the 1980s decked out in a white gown made of 180 white gloves, a white sash labeled "Mlle Bourgeoise Noir 1955" and a tiara on top of her head. It was a genius attempt to show the tony art world just how hypocritical, racist and elite they were, despite their gestures of goodness. O'Grady took performance and turned it against her audience, putting them on blast. She threw in their faces how many of them were unwitting participants and perpetrators in upholding a culture that valued oppression and palatable Black art and denied real expression and opportunity to artists who needed it most and whose voices the art world needed the most—the Black and brown, the women, the misfits, the wronged and maligned in the world. O'Grady wanted to wreak havoc in those rooms. Loud and indignant, she injected unpopular politics to transform these art-world rooms and shatter the facades of innocence and meritocracy that the cultural power brokers and gatekeepers hid behind. She broke decorum, said the quiet things out loud and took no prisoners.

So, as she moved through the Just Above Midtown and New Museum of Contemporary Art gallery space crowds, she'd occasionally stop in front of someone. Each time she'd say "Help me relieve my burden" and hand them one of the full-lipped white chrysanthemums from the bouquet she carried. By the time she finished handing them out, the bouquet would turn out to be a cat-o'-nine-tails, a whip used for punishing enslaved and imprisoned people.

I love the idea of imagining O'Grady practicing becoming Mlle Bourgeoise Noir in a bedroom mirror like me trying to transform myself into a rapper.

In photos of her as Mlle Bourgeoise Noir, you can see her smiling as she grooves around art gallery spaces, sometimes staring directly into the eyes of some of the white art-world gatekeepers, forcing them to confront how often their acceptance for Black art and artists was based on narratives and representations around Black suffering, slavery and survival. It was an amazing, bold move because it meant that they literally couldn't look away, and keeping her gaze and keeping the good humor of a performance that they probably found socially awkward forced them to consent to the blame she placed in front of them. Mlle Bourgeoise Noir was also O'Grady's challenge to the same Black art and artists that rested on the laurels of what the white art world would accept, too, though—she knew that they could do better; we had far more to offer. The Mlle Bourgeoise Noir persona also doubled as a mirror for the Black artists who she felt secured their space in the art world by molding their work and their artistic choices to fit its narrow palette and limited vision of the boundaries of what Black artists could engage with in their work. It's because of *that* feeling that O'Grady also proclaimed:

THAT's ENOUGH!
No more *boot*-licking . . .
BLACK ART MUST TAKE MORE RISKS!!!

O'Grady's approach as Mlle Bourgeoise Noir reminds me of the battle rapper, of the sort of call-out culture meant to reignite and even reinvent a space.

O'Grady's 1980 to 1983 Noir appearances left a legacy of bravery and brilliance. One artist who followed in her footsteps was a 2010-era Kanye West, who used the promotion of his upcoming album *My Beautiful Dark Twisted Fantasy* as a sort of cultural passport to show up at the *Rolling Stone* and Facebook offices, two culture-defining places that he felt weren't seriously appreciating Black art. Kanye performed unreleased songs on boardroom tables and conference stages. He sat with editors and programmers to discuss how limited and limiting hip-hop had become, and his desire to "bring [rap] to another level," seeing himself as the latest in a long line of cultural truth tellers burdened with pushing society forward. Kanye did all this in a sort of photo-negative version of O'Grady's Noir persona; he was dressed like a cross between a G-man, Will Smith in *Men in Black* and a pallbearer. All-black suit and tie, black sunglasses.

Kanye made his case as if he was a barbarian beating at the gates of white appreciation and acceptance. His frustrations around hip-hop, largely read as a Black genre, and its stagnation were similar to O'Grady's sentiments about the art world and everyone complicit in it. And the Kanye act—of being outspoken, out there and out of control—felt like an extension of his argument that hip-hop had suddenly found itself as neither respected nor innovative anymore. It angered West that the genre felt like it was under siege and undervalued. He knew that the music and artistry still had so much more they could say and do, and so he went around pushing all of this, all of us, further. While those pushes at the time came from a similar place as O'Grady's, present-day Kanye is now a persona composed of dark-corner Reddit and Twitter/X threads, and his once-clear manifesto about what art, Black identity, politics or even hip-hop means has become indecipherable to everyone, maybe even himself.

O'Grady's legacy also shone through three years later through Kendrick Lamar's "Control" verses. Lamar's words were also a callout to hip-hop, his bars calling for the return of competition between emcees. He felt the loss of this art had watered down the ferocity, creativity and urgency in hip-hop. He lay down the same kind of challenge that O'Grady did, demanding that his peers get back on top of their shit. Lamar issued his challenge in hip-hop terms, though:

> What is competition? I'm tryna raise the bar high
> Who tryna jump and get it?

Lamar's bars might be loud and brash, but this is the way you have to crash the party, so to speak, and people in the culture understand that these sorts of moves are WWE-like: largely tongue-in-cheek, hyperbolic bravado that's a splash of cold water in people's faces. It's playful but serious, daunting but communal, metaphoric and earnest.

Let me tell you a secret: I spent four years in high school as a rapper. My family and friends didn't know about it. No one at school had any idea, either. But it was true; I spent years in my bedroom being a rapper. With MTV on or playing a CD on my multidisc stereo, I was Dre, Snoop, Ice Cube, every member of Tribe and the Fugees. In my bedroom mirror, I pantomimed and perfected rap posture, and I learned to copy their voices and their cadences. I came up with new performances each time, creating fictional settings and routines to "Let Me Ride," "Gin and Juice," "Scenario." I didn't even always understand what I was rapping—I didn't know what it meant to rhyme "Bust off on your couch, now you got Seaman's Furniture." And when I studied the videos, just as much as I was looking at the women in them, I was studying the rappers, locating where they found a confidence, a swagger, a power that made it possible to walk through the kind of city streets, empty playgrounds and groups of other Black boys and men that I'd see around town.

I wanted to understand how I could go to school the next day, walk the halls and sit at the desks with the same fearlessness as the boys around me. I wanted to be able to change in the locker room and not worry about how my half-naked body was just going to confirm I was an easy mark for the others. I wanted to understand what I could do, who I could be, in order to survive the gauntlet of shame I experienced daily on the bus rides home, where the other boys—the boys who could rap and feel like IRL rappers—would bully me and the other misfits.

And as a Black boy constantly surrounded by white classmates, I wanted proof that I was still Black. In a roundabout way, that's how I came to understand the power of a Black performance. I learned it through watching the magnetic pull that hip-hop was having on everyone around me. It seemed to bend reality and make other people around us uncomfortable, and felt like its own secret language. It created a bit of a force field around you, making it hard for people to pierce those parts of you that you wanted to protect.

In the '90s, while other people were still trying to make sense of rap, our generation was eating it up like cereal. We loved the storytelling, the imagery, the metaphor, the rhyme. Rap introduced us to the idea of freestyling, which meant language creation, which meant rule breaking, which meant competition, which meant identity, which meant persona, which meant genius. And we're so lucky to have those among us still keeping the old flame going, taking advantage of any and every situation to keep our cultural flame alive.

And some of these performances can transport you back to another time.

Shawn gives me a rap studio masterpiece during a Lyft ride through West Philly the day after the Fourth of July in 2023. When I get into his cream-colored Chevy Malibu, his thumping speakers are more like a time machine, blasting EPMD and Mobb Deep. My teeth rattle all the way back to my middle school years, hearing older boys effortlessly rapping on the bus. Without even realizing it, I am nodding my head before I've even put on my seatbelt.

He asks, "You OK with this?" as he half looks back, and when I mumble yes, he pulls the Malibu out of park. I can see he's wearing a sleeveless shirt, and on his arm there's a black ink tattoo of a microphone with a rat's tail of a curling cord underneath it.

On a ride from West Philly to Fairmount, my Lyft driver Shawn raps from the front seat. Photo courtesy of Tre Johnson.

When his muscle flexes, the mic moves like it's being invisibly gripped by a hand.

In no time Shawn's also telling me his story. He's forty-eight, with a couple of kids in their late teens and early twenties who're into mumble rap instead of what we're listening to right now.

They're not into Shawn's personal history with rap; he tells me about the years he's spent competing in open mic competitions around Philly and Delaware and being on the road opening for white rock bands with his own original music. He still spends time in the studio working on rap "for the love of the music," he tells me, and still pops into any open mic competition so he can "show I can still come off the bench and drop 40."

When Shawn reaches to switch on Spotify, he surprises me by putting on some of his own music from an album under his name, Shawn Major, called 1975, the year his dad graduated from high school. And then for the remainder of my ride with him, he blasts 1975 at full tilt in the car, rapping and flexing along with every line and track that he can play for me for the next fifteen minutes. His entire being transforms in front of me during that stretch; Shawn's rapping is time machine, tutelage, showing off for an invisible crowd in this Chevy Malibu.

We're a rolling studio, a mobile concert, and every grunt and flex he gives to the music, he's giving to me, too. He's reminding me rap is an incantation. I'm totally spellbound by Shawn's voice and how hip-hop's Black storytelling is a construct of history, biography, politics and place. Wherever Shawn slips into in 1975, that place occupies 1975 as both his daddy's high school graduation year and, obviously, the same year Shawn was born. Because of that, Shawn's style of rap is a throwback—1975 sounds ambered in the 1990s with hard beats, samples and slang that's too stubborn to bow to what he calls today's "mumble rap." He's also trying to reach and hold on to a version of the Black music, masculinity and storytelling that's receding into the background as it gets swallowed up by time and the mainstream.

And even though folks like Shawn think it's been lost, I think a lot of hip-hop and rap's power in performance is still alive and well, even with the latest generations.

Have you ever walked down the street rapping out loud? Try it once and see how it feels. And do it with your chest; say the words out loud—out loud like you're having a conversation with someone walking next to you or on the phone. Loud enough for someone else to hear, loud enough to make out the words, loud enough to be seen. It's actually something that I see a lot of Black folks, young and old, do even now. I'll be walking through the city and see a Black boy riding down the block balancing a speaker in his hands or on the handlebars, zigzagging his way down the block. On the bus and the subway, especially in the last couple of years, people will play tracks over their phone on full volume. Their grips on the metal transit poles makes them look like they've casually slid into this reality and, at any moment, might jerk right back up the pole into hip-hop space. They meet your eyes and they dare anyone else to look back, sometimes pantomiming along with the songs in the same way Shawn escorted me through the city on that ride.

From my apartment windows, I've watched brothers walking

through Fairmount—a largely white, middle- to upper-middle-class neighborhood—rapping down the street. The joy of rapping is the joy of singing, and the joy of music in general is that when it hits you, you're bound to share it with others. Now, this is of course sometimes tricky because of the way that rap both continues to portray content—drug use, explicit sex, a general mixture of angst and anger and the demeaning of honestly damn near anyone—and market itself in the least family-friendly ways. It's still, however, maybe the most dominant sonic representation of many aspects of Black experiences in the world. Rapping in public's like a Black cultural whistle; it's the lyrics-based version of *The Wire*'s Omar, who himself felt like a throwback to cowboys strolling and beat cops whistling. It's a way of announcing yourself and taking up space—this tiny Black passport you carry around with you wherever you go, making sure you have a right to pass and stand in places. It's also a plain old booster; rapping out loud fills you up. Again, I'm telling you to just walk out your door one day and try it. Take your rap song into the street, say it out loud and watch the world blossom into Black technicolor all around you.

Yemi Abiade described the new drill genre in these terms: "Scratching beneath the surface of their explosive and territorial bravado further, you discover that these drillers are really crying out for help." He reminded folks that rap's often created in a cauldron where they're a part of "communities that are constantly being let down by cuts to local services, such as youth clubs and school services" in his 2018 essay "Inside UK Drill, the Demonised Rap Genre Representing a Marginalised Generation." In its own way, this rapping is the same teen chaos energy of flash mobs, just at a smaller, more intimate scale. It's the same jubilant reminder that these Black kids exist, expressing an awareness of the discomfort their mere existence sometimes provokes in both Black and non-Black people mixed with a bit of IDGAF.

But also, this shit is just fun. Rapping in public's fun. Rapping at work is fun. Rapping on the train or the bus, in the car with your friends? Fun. And that sort of fun is an emotional lubricant when you're walking through the world. There's been times that I've been rapping down the street and another Black person recognizes the song, or the act of hearing me rap out loud makes me more visible to them. Might get a small head nod or greeting in those moments, like an invisible dap as we pass by each other.

So go ahead and rap when you're out and about. Put your chest out. Let them know you're here.

Walk up to spaces.

Own the space.

See the door.

Kick in the door.

✧ ✧ ✧

Towards the end of season two of HBO's corporate family wealth drama *Succession*, we get a treat: At a gala celebrating the family patriarch, Logan Roy, his oldest son, Kendall, takes the stage in front of the crowd. Slightly bent over the mic, he speaks a few words and then he opens his mouth to perform a rap tribute, as his buttoned-up, Dinner Attire Fun Kendall sheds his corporate shell to unleash an inner persona, rocking the kind of customized sports jersey you'd buy at a mall kiosk. His younger brother, Roman, mockingly calls him "Ken.W.A" (try reading it out loud), and when he starts rapping, there's the slightest shift in his body and voice. For a minute, to the horror of both the show's audience and the dinner crowd, Kendall slips into a cringeworthy original rap that's done without irony. The scene works because it's a familiar kind of cultural cosplay a lot of us have probably encountered; there's a real steep, sometimes awe-inspiring audacity to white folks rapping, not just because rap is Black-formed but also because, as a result, it's intrinsically Black-etho'ed. While Kendall's not doing anything stranger than a lot of us who've imagined ourselves as rappers (or even rappers who've fictionalized their artist identity to sell us their music), it's still the type of performance that feels like cultural Blackface. Obviously, white rappers also roam the hip-hop realms, to largely mixed results. For most cultural observers like myself, only a handful of the white ones succeed in not seeming like they're rapping as a means to cash a check or as a way of disrespecting Black culture. Acts like Eminem, Mac Miller and Action Bronson, and maybe newer ones like Jack Harlow, have stuck the landing on honoring hip-hop culture by blending elements of regionality, narrative, voice and a respect for the genre's origins.

That *Succession* scene took place in the episode titled "Dundee," which aired in 2019, and for at least twenty years prior to that people have been critiquing hip-hop's flirtation with white and corporate America. Nancy Jo Sales's 1999 *Vibe* piece "Money Boss Player" reads like a cringeworthy exposé observing the blurring lines between race, power and money vis-à-vis rappers and Donald Trump. While watching Black music moguls like Andre Harrell, Puff Daddy (nowadays also known as Diddy) and Russell Simmons partying in Manhattan, she highlights the ways that a mutual affection was growing not just between these figures but also between rap and (white) corporate America. Throughout the piece, Sales points out the envies and overlaps; a choice passage mentions Trump's cameo on Method Man's 1998 album *Tical 2000: Judgment Day* in the eleven-second track "Donald Trump (Skit)." She goes on to quote Meth about The Donald: "I like Trump's style. It's like 'I'm rich, fuck y'all. I build my buildings and put my name on them. Fuck y'all.'" Throughout it all, Trump is blithely clueless about the whole rap scene, claiming he doesn't "even listen to rap," but enamored with the camaraderie. While it might be hard to picture Trump ever having a Kendall moment, you can imagine him sitting in the audience enjoying a rap serenade from Donald Trump Jr., his big head nodding with smug approval.

Rap's defenders have always had a complicated relationship with the genre—often even the heights of hip-hop are still marred with flecks of misogyny, violence, drug-trade tales and materialism, sometimes in the same set of bars. This provides rap's biggest detractors with evidence of why so much of the genre needs to be eliminated or at least less celebrated.

But for all the indignation that the music supposedly inspires, the biggest culprits for this are considerably less examined. After all, it's the corporate world's own violent language of "layoffs," "downsizing," "recalibrating," "right-sizing" that has the sort of real-world implications that not only allow but arguably produce the cauldron that rap's created in. Through their mergers, takeovers, efficiencies, pivots and strategic rollouts, American corporations and banks routinely create the cooking pot where Americans are boiled alive, and then shake down and crush them to find the best sediments that will maximize profits and company value for executives, stakeholders and board members

That's not to give rap a pass, but ignoring the irony of Kendall and the Roys admiring the world of rap while also largely being responsible for what kind of rap is made—while *also* heavily profiting from it through media and politics—is dizzying. These are profit-first executives whose practices are eroding our community—redlining and discriminatory bank loans, development projects that displace us, exploitative social media platforms and tech companies, and privatization efforts that create posh real estate and construction deals for the rich while demolishing public schools. People want to talk about how entities like Cash Money, Death Row, Def Jam and No Limit have been ruining the Black community, when they're only repercussions of the names we should be talking about: DeVos, Sackler, Sinclair and Murdoch. These record labels are merely a slice of the cabal of companies and conservatives that have found ways to place Black life under the heel of American society. Ask them to take the stage and rap romantically about manufacturing the housing, job, opioid, mental health and policing crises.

As these multibillionaires profit off Black labor, the fact that rap has continued to talk about reaching the same pinnacle of this type of capitalist excess and influence is not proof of the existence of an American Dream but a revelation of how unreachable that goal is.

Black culture has been America's favorite shopping catalog since way before they dreamt up having Kendall rap on stage.

In 2018 my old college friend Crystal Oliver invited me to St. Mary's College of Southern Maryland, where she'd been teaching undergrad courses on song lyrics and poetry. She brought me there to talk about race and music, and while I visited campus I always felt on edge; some people told me ahead of time that the county had a long history with the Klan, and to this day, on and off campus, there was a lot of backwards, racist thinking. Still, I came; Crystal was someone I adored, and I looked forward to the chance to talk music and culture with some of the St. Mary's students.

After spending a day or two in small discussion groups and giving an evening keynote to some of the St. Mary's students and faculty, I sat in Crystal's office reminiscing and talking shit on my last day. Before I left, though, she handed me something. "Take this," she said. "It's something that I've had for a bit, but I feel like you'll know what to do with this."

She reached towards her shelf and handed me a thin, faded green booklet titled *Old Cabin Home Minstrels: A Minstrel Entertainment in Three Acts*. The cover was designed with a hand-drawn illustration of a rural Black family living in a cabin home set in the backwoods, each person situated somewhere between the front porch and the patchy front lawn, where they danced juba and played the banjo. They're all drawn smiling with the same large, white framing around their mouths, exaggerating their lips.

Early twentieth century white female composer Carrie B. Adams concocted *Old Cabin Home Minstrels*, released by the now-defunct Lorenz Publishing in 1921, from old slave songs and one-dimensional Black stereotypes. *Old Cabin Home* is a wicked three-act spell book full of incantations with a combination of characters—"Aunt Dilly," "Lily Vi'let," "Uncle Toby," "Sambo," the choir of "eight little pickaninnies"—and Negro songs that white performers could conceivably use to transform themselves into the Black figures on the cover.

Adams's cultural liner notes give lots of guidance. "Careful rehearsals," she notes, will lend themselves to "spur of the moment" improvisations that would, in essence, mirror the "moving music [of] the old slave songs, where everyone is inspired to move in rhythmical sequence." The instructions stress that there "must be no stiffness and no standing still," and as the lead characters, "Aunt Dilly" and "Uncle Toby" are described as needing to be "rather large."

The larger problem lies in what continues to corrupt Black performances, though. In the activism sphere, while there's been a resurgence of everyday, visible actions, its impact has also been hampered by colliding with today's social media and brand culture. This has turned the type of earnest performance activism—even when it's been cringey—into a series of skeptical, inauthentic gestures. Post-2016, with the rise of Donald Trump, as movement activism became popular, so, too, did the rise of artificiality, preening for celebrity status and a desire to have "a platform." That created a vortex of performances that diluted social messages and movements, shifting what were once performances intended to provoke and disrupt into a series of orchestrated and superficial moves and actions that seem way more interested in aiming for virality, followers and brand endorsements.

Nowadays, if people are doing something disruptive and provocative, there's a good chance it's for the algorithms. That's something that's tainted a lot of activist spaces and conversations and doesn't seem to be going away, especially as Black and non-Black people alike have found ways to translate their access to Black inequality and justice conversations into everything from book deals to podcasts, cable network appearances and apparel.

These activists are not provoking rooms in the ways that O'Grady or Gregory did during their times, or even imagining unorthodox ways of pushing perception or politics like Kevin Hart. No Black performer or activist wants to feel alone in the room dogged by the question "Nigga, is you crazy?"

Before his comeback, one of Dave Chappelle's initial reappearances was on a 2008 episode of *Inside the Actors Studio*. Sitting across from James Lipton, Chapelle opened the episode snickering, "Everybody's waiting to see how crazy I am." He'd been gone from the public eye for several years after famously exiting *Chappelle's Show* at its height and leaving $50 million behind. In that interview, he shared an anecdote about Martin Lawrence's infamous 1996 incident standing in the middle of a freeway waving a gun. "The worst thing to call somebody is 'crazy'—it's dismissive," he said.

Ultimately, our Black performance, when leveraged for safety, is complicated. It can put you square in society's sights if you're too disruptive, and yet you chance leaving behind and mortgaging something of your dignity and your cause when you're too compliant, accommodating or malleable. It's no longer in vogue to be a platformed disruptor in today's culture; now we're way more focused on getting seats at the table or making them, than dismantling the table itself. That's fine; that, too, requires a certain ingenuity and nimbleness to skirt danger.

Right on cue, my nephew, who's not even twelve years old yet, can transform into Michael Jackson. I mean pretty full-on, too; he can slide into the same leathery-smooth footsteps, those same herky-jerky movements. His little brow clouds over as he concentrates, and his brain—full of Mega Man villain names, the chronological casting of the It and Spider-Man franchises—selects the right file for an MJ routine. He knows the moves in every music video, even ones like MJ's '96 song "Ghosts"; music from long after I'd stopped listening to him. And what I love is that he doesn't just do this out of love for MJ's moves and art-istry, but by inhabiting MJ, he's able to do a couple of things. He can find an escape from the daily bullying and harassment he gets at school, from the stresses at home that he can't do any-thing about. He can, most definitely, give us joy with his panto-miming; it's so earnest, so precise, so practiced and so aware that his performing these dance numbers—in my parents' living room, in the corner of my sister's house in front of the TV—just makes us so happy, so giddy. He dances and you can't help but feel lighter looking at this little boy who loves so many things—the love for dance, the joy of obsession, the comfort of routine and control in an absolutely bonkers world.

His body's a time machine and a diary in those moments. He carves out a portal back to a time when it was easier to love MJ and we still marveled at the lithe ability of our Black heroes and how they moved through the world. My nephew is a living leg-acy, a boy who is unknowingly keeping a culture alive, who is al-ready learning how to use the past and his body to communicate with himself and the world around him. He's already learning, and I'm hoping that he'll continue to pull from his surroundings to create space, love, silence and reflection for himself and the people around him he loves. At some point, my sister got him an MJ outfit, so whenever he had the hat and glove nearby, he'd don them.

He doesn't look like Michael, but in those moments he's giving Michael, and that's enough to give each one of us joy, peace, a release, a memory-forming experience together. In these moments, my nephew dances somewhere between awareness of us and forgetting we're here, but when he spins on the carpet, I'm six years old again watching a young Black teen girl next to me faint at the sight of Michael Jackson stepping on stage at John F. Kennedy Stadium in Philly.

He twirls, and we're back to pre-pandemic times when we were always able to sit together like this, watching the kids be kids, laughing and talking together.

My nephew touches the brim of his MJ fedora and tucks his chin to his chest, and everyone we've lost and all the things we could still be are alive at once. In the magic of nostalgia, I see the imagination of our family and our culture's new future dancing in front of me.

He already sees how healing and transformative performing can be. As difficult as this country, school, money and society can be, somehow my nephew already understands and practices the cultural need to perform. Like a lot of us, he reconstitutes all the good and bad around him and—if only for a few minutes to the tune of "Remember the Time"—becomes something even more beautiful than he is every day. May that never leave him, like it's never left most of us. May he see and feel the magic and always know that this is available to him. That life as a Black man will continue to have moments of defeat and dehumanization, but also of dreams and destiny. That whenever he's in doubt about who or what is next for him, whenever there doesn't seem to be space for himself or others around him, he knows to find the file in his brain and conjure up a force field.

Hold those things, Neph.

Twirl again.

CHAPTER 6

Agitate! Agitate!

Black Paranoia™ and Surveillance

Stranger in Paris, France, as we made our way to the Sacré-Cœur on a visit to the city. Photo courtesy of Tre Johnson.

contracted Black Paranoia™ at fifteen years old delivering homework to one of my best friends in high school. This meant stepping into the white, working-class side of Pennington Road down by where we lived in Ewing Township, the small suburban area bordering the Jersey capital, Trenton. After I dropped the assignments off in her family's mailbox, two white male Ewing police officers stopped me before I could cross back over Pennington. In a flash, they had me face down on the hood of the police cruiser—I can still feel the engine's humming warming the left side of my cheek. Back then, the area around Greenland Avenue was a mainly Irish, Polish and Italian family neighborhood.

There'd been trouble around then, too; I remembered reading a *Trenton Times* blurb about a fight between some white guys who were hanging out at a neighborhood bar and chased a couple of young Black boys who were passing through, tossing bottles at them and ending up in a fistfight with a couple of them. Knowing us, those kids were probably headed to the Burger King over on Olden Avenue and used that neighborhood as a shortcut. Didn't matter, though; they were trespassers, which meant that I was trespassing on the day that I dropped off Jamie's schoolwork.

"What're you doing?" the closest officer asked.

I explained that I'd been dropping off homework to a friend, a classmate.

". . . in this neighborhood?" he asked, as he cocked his head to the side. We all knew what he meant.

I nodded and pointed to what suddenly felt like an imaginary house down Greenland Avenue as they searched me; one of the officers ran his hands along my back, my sides, between my legs. It was dusk; the sky was pinkening into cotton candy, which meant people were getting home from work and getting ready for dinner, and older retired white people were sitting on their porches.

"Hold still," said the officer, and so I held still. All I did was adjust my face, flipping it to rest on one side or the other, and opened and closed my eyes. When they were shut, it was because the officer's hands were roving over me. When they were open, I looked at the homes across the street; in the windows and on the porches, I could see white residents looking at me, their faces lit by their living room and porch lights, blushing when the still-flashing red cruiser lights slid over them.

Someone had obviously called the cops after watching me debate whether to leave the schoolwork against Jamie's front door or in her mailbox and deciding I was really probably trying to break into the house.

I was in such a walking coma that I didn't realize they'd taken my book bag off me until I heard it unzip and then plop somewhere on the cruiser near my head.

After they asked for my name and address, I cried on the

police cruiser's hood, mainly because I was mad at myself for being so stupid. I kept reciting all the "know betters" that I'd been taught about going places by myself or walking around white neighborhoods, or being friends with white kids in school.

This is your fault, I told myself. It's your fault you're going to be taken to juvie or jail, I said. They'll tell Mom that you did something wrong so they had no choice.

They let me go because, of course, there was nothing I'd actually done wrong that they could take me in for. But it felt like a warning: We're not taking you in this time, but just remember we're all watching. Whatever it was, after that I understood. When I got home, I didn't say anything to Mom about what happened. I didn't say anything to anybody, to be honest.

Not for a long time, and when I say a long time, I mean not until after college even. As a matter of fact, this might be Mom's first time hearing this story. Sorry, Mom. I'm good.

That was 1993. That's how I contracted my first case of Black Paranoia™.

Black Paranoia is the historical and cultural state of having been relentlessly surveilled. Black Paranoia can make some Black people guarded and avoidant and/or concerned with respectability politics, things like "sitting up straight" and "acting right," because these might help them avoid harm from the cops or gain more opportunities and access to things controlled by white people. Black Paranoia is the unshakable feeling you're being watched. Sometimes we're being watched by other Black people who're looking out for us—neighborhood adults, teachers and mentors, coworkers and friends—and sometimes we're being watched by people who are looking to get us.

A result of us being so heavily surveilled by society, Black Paranoia has been a gift and a curse of sorts. We've used it to create our own spaces, behaviors, language and intuition around the idea that we're being watched and need to have inventive skills to navigate this. We keep it in mind when we're shit talking and worried that someone's reading our messages; I used to be on a group text with two other nonwhite friends, and we had a numerical code we'd use to refer to white people so we didn't have to say "white people." I'm sure some of y'all have been like me, too; the set of senses you tap into when you decide to pull over at a restaurant or bar when you've been driving for a while but leave as soon as you step inside because you just know the vibes are off. Like the time I was driving from Houston, Texas, back home to Trenton and ended up eating my Outback dinner in a parking lot in the middle of Alabama because of all the stares I'd gotten when I walked in.

And while I learned a lot through that neighborhood incident as a teen, I don't think there was anything like what I learned when I worked for three years in Camden.

From 2014 to 2017 I worked in the Camden City School District Superintendent's Office for Paymon Rouhanifard, a young educator who'd been appointed by then-Governor Chris Christie as the latest part of New Jersey's state takeover of Camden. I'd joined the superintendent's office as part of his new administration after licking my wounds from my time as TFA's Philadelphia ED. Our job was, on the surface, to "fix" Camden's schools, which meant a mixture of closing schools and bringing in new charter schools. Getting there required some real gross cultural moves.

Camden's tiny; even though almost eighty thousand live there, it's basically a small town of churches, restaurants, homegrown small businesses, convenience stores and fast-food joints that most people could name off the top of their head. Most people seem to work for city hall, the school district or one of the many small businesses there. A handful of native Camdenites work at the Rutgers and Rowan campuses in town, but a lot of the prestige places like Campbell's soup and the Camden Waterfront, with its aquarium, concert space and corporate offices, employ people in the surrounding areas of Cherry Hill, Collingswood, Philly and Mount Laurel.

The town's one old supermarket had shuttered years before.

So jobs, good paying jobs, were scarce for people who lived in the city. When we all came in to work for Paymon, we were the latest wave of a 2013 workforce takeover happening right around the time Camden's police force had been overhauled with new police officers from outside the city—a process that ultimately didn't end until around 2017. A lot of those officers were like those of us in the superintendent's office, that mixture of outsider, non-Black or both. And together, both the education and the police takeovers—heavily composed of non-Camden individuals—created a surveillance bubble around Camden, meaning once you stepped into the city, someone or something was always watching you.

Part of the surveillance was technological. The software ShotSpotter placed a series of hidden microphones in the most notorious neighborhoods to triangulate a shooting incident within ten feet and instantly alert the police so officers could respond in rapid time—at times as fast as under thirty seconds. While the tech was new, ShotSpotter was actually just the latest in a long line of Camden surveillance. There were already two hundred police cameras, as well as a thirty-foot crane with a camera mounted on top that allowed it to scan half a dozen blocks. Governor Christie and Police Chief J. Scott Thompson both touted the use of surveillance technology as "effective" and saw Camden as a "model for other cities."

As newcomers and outsiders to Camden, it felt like we were part of that surveillance model. Even though I joined the superintendent's team to be closer to the community, schools and Black people again, I didn't realize that I'd be joining a sort of new elite. Coming from TFA, from anywhere other than Camden, being Black and familiar with Philly-Camden area, all worked in my favor as the type of someone who "got it" and was down for what the administration's agenda called for. And so in 2014 I started as the board liaison and community relations director in the superintendent's office.

This attitude was clear during the times that I hung out at after-work social gatherings with new administration people. They not only often looked down on the city and our veteran coworkers, they loved to watch and mock them. After attending a retirement party celebrating a veteran staff member's years of service, one white woman coworker shared her reaction to the scene while we had dinner together. "All I thought," she shared over wine, "was, For what?"

A lot of the social hangs outside of work were like this, people sharing their latest stories about how they watched or interacted with the Black veteran staff back in the office and schools. How these people talked, acted and worked. I faded from going to these hangs after a while; I started feeling like a cultural double agent caught between needing to be around these professional peers who usually didn't look, talk, think or act like me and being back in the office talking with my other Black coworkers.

Those initial months on staff were often confusing like that because I felt simultaneously outside and inside. Even though I'd been in the Philly-Camden area for eight years by then, I wasn't an actual Camden local or someone who'd spent enough time there to act much like I knew the place or any of the people. I'd done some school visits in the city thanks to my time on staff at Teach for America, but my only other times in the city were going to the Camden aquarium with my family when I was a kid and to the Glow in the Dark tour at the Camden Waterfront to see Kanye, Rihanna and N.E.R.D in 2007. So in that sense, I was another outsider, and because of the political capital that came with my professional network and connections, the new take-over staff—many of them a mix of white and non-Black people who came from NYC and Newark—was kinda the crew it was a good idea for me to run with whenever possible.

At the same time, though, even among the new crew I was one of a handful of visible Black folks. And the central office was still heavily, maybe even predominantly, Black, so when I showed up to work that first day, there was also a way in which I was almost immediately inside because I was Black, too. And once I (repeatedly) showed that I was down with the Black folks already there, I found my stride and felt inside and more at home. Because truthfully, I felt more at ease with and found it easier to navigate the Camden Black community I was working with than to deal with all the secret texting, back talking, inside jokes and cultural superiority cues that came with hanging out with the white-collar crew of TFA, NY Department of Education and education reform people.

Regardless of "veteran" or "new" status, as the Black staff

we would all trade notes about what we were hearing, seeing and being told.

Since these weren't conversations that we could have out in the open, we popped into each other's offices or went on walks together in pairs—never more than two—to grab lunch or coffee. On top of that, we were all aware of how many of us were being watched. Leadership members of the superintendent's cabinet, known as "chiefs," reported directly to Paymon while overseeing the key district departments. They would often pop by or casually hang around our offices after team or staff meetings, but also during the day, when the hallways maybe felt suspiciously quiet or when there was a din of socializing going on. It was also common for someone to say something like "I saw you having coffee with [insert name of person who made the administration nervous]" or monitor when you came and went from the office. For a while, some of us were certain that even our emails were being secretly monitored. The administration was cloaked in adolescent spy games. They had a "secret" email account that basically everyone knew about anyway, invite-only text threads discussing things (and currying internal political favor), and on more than one occasion, we learned our conversations were being either shared or eavesdropped on by someone else nearby.

Over time, the Camden central office felt like a coffin to a lot of us. Staff, particularly Black staff, were routinely being laid off, and we watched with horror as more and more outsiders—often young, white and connected—were brought in at positions and salaries higher than the rest of us. The entire place felt tight and depressing; the administration's smugness was a shovel, constantly heaping shit onto the rest of us. Morale sank lower and lower as time went on, schools were being closed and more and more staff were demoted or disappeared.

Gradually, the Black staff—new and old hires alike—began realizing how much we were being watched, how often our movements, conversations, friendships and acquaintances were being tracked by the administration. Black Paranoia set into the place in no time, but fortunately we stumbled on our own plan.

Fried Shrimp Wednesdays.

Fried Shrimp Wednesdays became our way of having closed-door conversations about the stress and the bullshit we were enduring working for the administration. My coworker Tanya, a beautiful human being who made it possible for me to survive all those years, loved being responsible for coordinating the lunch. She didn't care if you were mid-meeting, mid-email or mid-thought: come 10:00 a.m. or so on Wednesday, she'd be up in your face asking, "OK, what's your order?"

Black people from almost every floor in the central office would place an order for fried shrimp (or wings; someone would occasionally order wings) and once the order came in, everyone would come to the office Tanya and I shared, and we'd all huddle around the almost-room-sized conference table and talk.

Those lunches became a pocket universe where time and pain stopped. For the longest time, Fried Shrimp Wednesdays in our office were the only place to have conversations away from the paranoid, watchful eyes of the administration. Inside our office, under the cover of fried shrimp lunches, the Black staff that gathered together talked through everything. When Black people's death made national news, we would often sit around and talk about how we were feeling, drawing parallels to some of the situations we faced working in the central office.

There were times when people came in either already crying or ended up in tears sharing the latest stories about how they'd been treated by one of the Death Eaters (my nickname for Paymon and his chiefs).

I think more than a few times we stopped or saved people from quitting or being fired by talking out and coaching each other through situations that were pushing people to the edge.

A lot of times we were just cutting up, too, sharing stories, gossiping, teasing each other, talking about the ridiculousness of the schools and the district.

It became more than a sanctuary; it was also the space where we established a Black information system about the underhanded things we saw the administration do. We vetted the staff around us with each other, learned who was cool and who you had to watch out for. And instead of getting played by having decisions sprung on us, we started sharing everything we knew about firings, hirings and demotions ahead of time.

You have to understand—those were hard times. The air of being watched, of deep distrust, was thick as a piecrust. Black folks were let go or forced to retire seemingly overnight. There were days and months where you could hear the fear sitting in people's throats as we all shared the rumors circulating about layoffs and schools being shut down for good.

It was good while it lasted. After a while, some of the administration and even other staff members started catching on to something happening on Wednesdays, because the only thing more suspicious than Black folks being together is Black folks nowhere to be found. And a lot of us were popular, well-liked people in the building; folks wanted to be around us. So naturally, Fried Shrimp Wednesdays got infiltrated and gentrified just like every damn thing in Camden around then. Non-Black staff were trading their lil' yogurt and granola cups and bento boxes to get in on lunch. A couple of the Death Eaters, more likely interested in a combo of spying and looking like good bosses, started asking to place orders and sometimes hanging around during lunch.

What was funny was that they often approached the Camden food the same way they did Camden locals: cordially. Not engaging too much or too close but just enough to soothe their own discomforts and guilt. It was socially and politically expedient for people like the superintendent and various cabinet or near-cabinet-level folks to act the part of integrating, but as Black folks we knew that there were actually limits. Stepping into an overall cultural cocoon of fried shrimp from a local seafood joint eaten in a group setting of Black direct reports and administrative assistants hit different. That was unspoken, but we all knew and felt it.

Still, it wasn't too long before Fried Shrimp Wednesdays were over. The biggest thing I learned was to respect that Camdenites knew how to clock all of us—local, nonlocal, Black, white, brown, married, single, partnered, drunk, sober—and they always updated their whisper network that formal administration and powers couldn't decode or defeat. In such a small place, so many of the Black folks working in the district were relatives, best friends, play cousins, congregation members, neighbors, old lovers, older enemies, older-older friends. Some people literally grew up together, while others had worked together for decades, starting in the local schools together before making it to the central office. You'd figure out real quick that in a small city like Camden, yeah, Black folks might have jobs and titles and oversee programs or initiatives and whatnot, but so many of them were born and raised there—they'd been to each other's family birthday parties, baptisms, weddings, cookouts, funerals and reunions. The town brought to mind that Kendrick

Lamar's song "Hood Politics" from 2015's *To Pimp a Butterfly*: "Your homeboy, your block that you're from, boo-boo / lil' hoes that you went to school with, boo-boo." That feeling in Camden, that growing awareness as an outsider to that particular Black community that you were stepping into a place where everyone had history with each other. That's ultimately a hard thing for any power to beat.

So while various powerbrokers neurotically kept an eye on us, I don't think they often realized how so many local Black folks weren't new to the game. They'd already figured out how to be publicly cordial enough to not arouse suspicion when privately they were so close they gave each other rides, picked up each other's kids or had side hustles outside of work together.

You started seeing it; despite constant chaos in and around Camden, these were Black folks who had managed to find ways to survive the onslaught of changing administrations, political misfortunes, mob bosses, policies and funding situations. The city might've often found itself caught between a rock and a hard place, but folks there also knew how to catch each other once shit passed through.

And with good reason. In a town with local political mob bosses like George Norcross, and both local activists and antagonists on the street constantly watching who was with who where and when, there was a culture of being on edge and uneasy about relationships. It felt like everyone was wired, and if you made the wrong move and disturbed a thread with someone in Camden's political and social spiderweb, the whole thing quivered.

Informally, as the school board liaison my job was often to help figure out how to respect that culture, while also learning how to work within it.

And that was best tested through tending to Camden's advisory school board, a collection of fascinating personalities and paranoias. If the superintendent's cabinet were the Death Eaters, then the advisory board, to use another fantasy-world metaphor, were the Ringwraiths, a nine-member board comprised of individuals who represented different Camden fiefdoms. They were split between races—basically half Black and half Latino, with the exception of one white woman. My job, among other things, was to spend time getting to know them and be a bit of an errand boy for their questions and requests about district policies, communication, rumors, hirings and decision-making. So I spent time doing an assortment of things with them to get the job done, partying at parent council functions with Martha Wilson, driving board president Mrs. Blackshear around when she needed to run errands and ask me things privately. With the younger ones, like Taisha and Felicia, I'd visit them at their houses or offices, or chat with them over the phone while I walked downtown Camden. Stately businessman Jose Brito Bueno would have short and warm but professional phone calls with me, his otherwise public silence really a mask for a lot of deep thinking about schools, community and corruption that we'd quietly chat about. The lone white board member, Ms. Coscarello, was a former teacher in the district and loved to call me up on the phone and cuss me out.

The other Black women, like Ms. Atwood and Ms. Burley, were some of my favorites to talk to, mainly because their very strong IDGAF vibes, unique to each of their personalities, meant that we pushed away the bullshit and got down to business, talking real shit about what was often going on around us, even if there wasn't a whole lot we could do about it. Still, they were Camden's nine Nazgûl, the Ringwraiths who were largely powerless in light of the takeover.

And Camden being Camden, each one had their own way of addressing their paranoia; Ms. Burley loved talking to me in code over the phone and insisting on hand-delivered documents— never email. She didn't trust the district email or district-issued cell phones, and while the latter might've felt like more of a stretch, the former had some teeth to it.

"They," she'd say, referring to the administration, "are good for telling you half the information without thinking you don't realize you're only getting half."

Mrs. Blackshear, the advisory board head, loved a private conversation, so she'd have me take her on rides around Camden or meet her in a cramped closet-sized office over at the housing organization's offices, or sometimes just sit curbside outside of a random building.

But the best example was the time advisory board member Brother Minister Wasim Muhammad took me on an unexpected ride-along through Camden. Born and raised in the city, back in the day he was known as Donnie Walker, the starting guard who famously led Camden High School's undefeated basketball team. Over time, he joined the Nation of Islam (NOI) and spent years reinvesting in the city through a mixture of jobs, food, community and security—all things that a lot of Camdenites needed one way or another at times, or knew someone who did or would.

Brother Minister Muhammad has a tall, long-limbed body, a boyish face and, to this day, the quietly intense eyes still capable of picking apart defenses and running the fastbreak like he did on that 1986 Camden High School state championship team. The whisper network that shared fleeting information about people that other people saw you interacting with in Camden had already told me some things about Brother Wasim. I'd heard about his wives, his children. Heard about the oversight that he's got with the local NOI scene and his various power moves. I'd heard about an almost split nature of his persona. Everyone respected Brother Wasim, but no one wanted to fuck with Donnie Walker.

Or maybe it was the other way around depending on how you knew him.

"Want a ride back, young man?" Brother Minister Muhammad loved calling me "young man" or "young sir," followed by a slight bow and a firm handshake where he'd look me directly in the eyes, always holding my gaze.

I took him up on the offer despite it being a relatively short walk; I basically looked for any excuse to spend time getting to know each board member, and we'd just finished a community meeting at one of the local temples in town. Stepping onto the sidewalk, I was aware of that same sensation that I'd always had walking around Camden; people on every block were watching. All around the temple's perimeter, suited NOI men stood guard, warmly greeting people as they entered and exited the building. I noticed how quietly these brothers milled about, some of them standing stoically at attention and looking around the block, while others acted indifferent, but you knew that they were watching out of the corners of their eyes.

That's one of the great features of Black Paranoia, that almost mystical ability to be constantly aware of your surroundings with a sliver of your retina never failing to watch from the side. And on the block, in the streets, in the office, you were always watching, watching, watching, mainly because you know that someone else was potentially watching, watching, watching you, too. As we made our way to Brother Muhammad's black sedan, brought over to us by one of the brothers, I looked at its sleek, un-scuffed exterior, and before we stepped into the car, I looked around both explicitly and out of the corner of my eye.

The ride should've been a quick one, ten minutes tops, to the Broadway PATCO stop. A couple of turns and we should've been there. But Brother Wasim Muhammad and I were cruising through Camden in his dark, sleek car like a Black Batman and Robin. And the whole time, he's partially leaned over like he's advising me in court as my legal counsel, close enough that our shoulders sometimes touch. And he's schooling me, telling me everything that I need to know about Camden, Camden streets, Camden people.

I'm in this car to learn; we both agree about that. As we hit corners and stop at traffic lights, Brother Muhammad is doing several things at once: He's pointedly watching the sidewalks as we slide by, sometimes giving a swift, mayoral wave whenever he and someone else recognize each other. I can tell he's making note of things that I'll probably never understand or that would fly under my ignorant radar. He's also watching me, looking at me, sometimes intently, checking to see what kind of Black I might be. That's what Brother Muhammad's ride-along was about.

As we spun through the streets, he was in my ear, and he was pointing—I looked at his long, thin finger animatedly pointing so hard at the Camden scenery it could've poked a hole into the front windshield.

"You see," he said to me as we zipped through downtown, passing by the CVS and under the shadow of Cooper University

Hospital and swung by the tiny ECO Charter School. "You see, the Black community has lost its way. And you can see it in Camden—do you feel me, young man?"

"Yes, sir."

I looked out the window thinking about what Black folks were contending with here—the abandoned homes; the eerily empty stretches of blocks; the tired, sleepy, heavy bodies of brothers slumped on stoops. Police cars that sat so long and so still on some blocks that you'd have thought that they were lawn ornaments.

"The Black community, the Black man, needs to be able to have determination on his fate, his family, his community. The Black community, the Black man needs to be able to prosper without the contamination of interlopers of any and all types, the ones that know everything about us, from this"—he pointed to his head—"to this"—he pointed to his heart—"and this"—and with that same long finger, he circled his entire body.

"So, when you have invited or uninvited guests into your body, into your community, into your home, you always need to be aware at what cost it might come to this" (points again to head), "this" (points again to heart) "and this" (gestures again around his body).

After he finished, he kept his eyes on me. I swear the car must've been driving itself at this point.

This ride should've been a short one, but it occurred to me

that Brother's car was more like a rolling office, and that even he, for all that he'd amassed and built and meant for the city, still felt unsafe to say some things, to have some conversations, outside of his own car in a city crawling with mics, cameras and eyes and ears. As a result, for people like Brother Wasim and a number of others, it was important to figure out how much I was watching and paying attention, and who I was doing it for, and what I was doing with it and, crucially, how—how, how—did it mean whether I was aligned with The Cause (Black) or The Job (not Black, not Camden).

The car felt tight and hot after a bit, and by the time we got to the station I had absorbed so much that I felt stuffed and paranoid. I was less afraid of Camden, but I was re-enlightened about being aware.

Before I got out of the car, we exchanged a hard, firm handshake, and without being told, I knew that one of the final important things after all that was to make sure that I looked him back in the eye and didn't break contact until he did. I remember breathing hard when I got to the station entrance. Evening was coming up just as I was going down the escalator to get on the commuter train and head back to Philly. When I sat down, I kept opening and closing a text to Muhammad, thinking that maybe I should thank him for the ride and the talk, but that felt corny. I decided to turn off my phone screen just as the train emerged from the tunnel and raced by the city's two-worded, graffiti-style welcome sign that said "City Invincible."

That ride-along with Brother Minister Muhammad, the closed-door Fried Shrimp Wednesdays, the whispering and clandestine meetings in cars and the constant, and I mean constant, checking and sense of being checked on reminded me how bewildering it can be to figure out how to move inside our communities. The advantage of a place like Camden was that, no matter what, there were always going to be some places and people, and people in places, that outsiders, especially non-Black ones, couldn't ever access.

During that time in Camden, a lot of us found ourselves banding together on the sheer basis of being Black. The political and office-place climate made connecting hard, though; it was sometimes difficult to know who to trust. The heads of the superintendent's administration and the city's power brokers maintained that unease by creating that tension. People around us were suddenly either promoted or fired, new people were brought on from the outside with higher salaries and outside consultant groups swooped in to handle focus-group conversations, communications and city strategies, often pushing a lot of us away from the action. Camden was always a special place, but during the mid-2010s it felt extra odd thanks to whispers of Democrat mob bosses having folks killed and holding closed-door conversations, schools quietly being tagged for closing and, once again, the constant threat of being watched. All of this tainted how all of us Black folks were caught up in this situation, sometimes ending up tiptoeing around each other or needing to watch what we said. People were scared for their jobs, their money, their pensions—and even though most of us knew it was only a matter of time before the current superintendent's administration would pack up and move on, it was impossible to know when that would be for sure.

That's what made all those secret spaces and moments feel so valuable and important—it was not just the bonding and intel trading that happened there; we understood the necessity of cultural, professional, relational survival. Over time, the shenanigans reminded a lot of us that our fates were collectively tied under the same bullshit politics, power and people.

That Camden experience reminded me of Richard Pryor's thoughts in his autobiography *Pryor Convictions* about traveling along the Black Belt, where "there were no booking agents or managers who got you jobs . . . performers traded information among themselves." This meant that the workers told each other about "the club owners who was good, bad and indifferent, who liked to drink, fight, gamble, do drugs, and shit like that." We had a Camden Black Belt.

These methods aren't even back channels; they are the channel. And while a lot of people would sneer at how often coworkers seemed to get jobs because they were related and connected—despite very often doing their own version of the same, and continuing to do so—what it maybe most often spoke to was their inability to control or anticipate power and access. So we stuck together. For all the things that working in Camden could potentially culturally provide us with, being there and hanging out in the community, or patronizing their restaurants and businesses, visiting their churches, still wouldn't make us Blacker or more authentically Camdenites.

Thanks to the presence of everyday tech in people's lives, from home-security accessories like Ring to social apps like Nextdoor, Neighbors and Citizen, everyone has the ability to watch each other. This, of course, is the worst for us. We've been the most heavily screwed over thanks to tech that's not only deputized everyday citizens into community cops but also part-nered software developers with law enforcement on these rela-tively new devices, which has made it even easier for cops to surveil people.

A lot of people don't want to be judged for wanting to pro-tect their property, loved ones, deliveries or safety, but it's dis-ingenuous to ignore the idea that racial bias, even among Black people, works to our disadvantage. More and more, our neigh-borhoods are becoming their own little Camdens with a series of unblinking, recording, cold, watchful eyes peeking out of ev-ery home and dog whistles on every neighborhood app.

Not everyone's lured by this technology, though. English professor Chris Gilliard, a Black Detroiter who was born and raised in the city during the 1970s and '80s, has become a critical voice in conversations about tech, race and surveillance. He's written warnings in *The Washington Post*, *Slate* and *The Atlantic* about the dangers of hidden racial prejudice inside of what he calls "luxury surveillance" devices like Alexa, Fitbits, Apple Watches and other seemingly innocuous monitoring gadgets. When it comes to doorbell devices like Ring, he points out the similarly fatal flaws to ShotSpotter and Google's AI software Gemini, and the identification and surveillance strategies that have a long history in Black communities. Gilliard, along with tech scholars like Safiya Noble (author of 2018's *Algorithms of Oppression*), has detailed how these various "smart" (ShotSpotter, Gemini) and "luxury" (Ring, Alexa) devices are replete with cultural and technical design malfunctions that allow for bad practices and results. Those range from Google search results that spit out pornographic content when people search for "Black girls" online to the historical inaccuracy generated when Gemini produced images of Nazis who were rarely white-presenting. As leading Black voices on technology, race and cultural impact, Noble and Gilliard quickly point to the recurring harm that comes with the glossy promotion of this technology as smart, efficient and knowledgeable and the implicit signaling that it is fair, meritorious, inclusive and ethical. Misidentified

Black folks get harassed, arrested and even shot thanks to approaches and devices like these, which have little evidence of really working.

The convenience of these devices is what makes the habit of using them so hard to break. You might be reading or listening to this on some device right now or asking Echo to turn down the volume so you can focus on reading. It's easy to think, What's the harm? The notion of invisible tracking, a million electronic eyes probing our every move, doesn't feel that unnerving because there's no discernible harm felt. After all, the thinking goes, if you're not doing anything wrong and don't have anything to hide, what's the big deal about being watched? It's hard to step outside of the fascination with and appreciation of what these things give us—who doesn't want to know how many steps or screen time hours, or have music, movie and food suggestions at a glance? What's the big deal?

Picture this: Somewhere in America right now, a Black boy's walking down a neighborhood street at sundown. The sky's a rosy pink as he makes his way past the various houses along the block. Each time he passes one, a silent Ring records his movements and sends them off to a database. As someone spots him from their home-office window, they reach for their phone and open an app to send a message—"There's a teen walking around the block now looking suspicious—anyone else see him?"—that receives several Likes and a few replies like "Saw him too" and

"Can anyone tell what he's doing?" It's a block that he's not on very often, so he's only somewhat familiar with it. He's moving quickly but carefully as he looks from mailbox to mailbox. To calm his nerves, he's rapping out loud, just loud enough to be heard but not so loud that his voice slides under the front doors. He adjusts his backpack occasionally and doesn't stop moving until he reaches one particular house. In this time, about four other Rings have recorded him, and at least three residents have uploaded pics that they took of him on their camera phones, sharing them to different apps where they're in active threads about people coming through the neighborhood.

At the same time, someone at the grocery store checks their phone as they receive notifications on an app and remembers a recent incident that they'd read about. They respond, "I heard someone's been walking around stealing packages recently." More Likes as someone else chimes in agreeing. "Yeah, it happened to me last week," they respond. By the time that this young boy has turned to head up the block, he's no longer a boy: He's a suspicious prowling burglar that's broken into every car that's been molested on the block, pilfered every Amazon package that's gone missing despite showing "delivered," vandalized every home that's ever been disturbed. He's gone from fifteen years old to twenty-five or thirty, and his height's gone from five feet five to a menacing, indescribable "big." His nondescript, unremarkable outfit is suddenly the distinct, graphically illustrative description "a dark jacket, jeans, Nikes and a book bag of some sort," and now every one of those items feels like it's hiding a gun. Another commenter known for making rude remarks chimes in to say "Better hurry up before the activists run in to protect him," and while this comment bothers some of the others, at the same time people are thinking about their packages, their car, their stoop plants. No one wants to lose any of that.

By the time he's midway home, someone who only just got home and is catching up on the conversation on one of these apps recognizes the boy from a distance and yes, from here he looks like he's in his late twenties, might be carrying something, and could be looking to cause more trouble. They alert the police, who are already patrolling the area anyway as one of the officers has their own account on a similar app. Before long, they're quietly tailing him. They decide to turn on the cruiser lights and stop him before he gets any farther.

As he lies face down on the hood of the police cruiser, he'll think about all the things he's been told about walking alone. He'll remember how earlier in the day he spent time talking to other kids in his classes about how the city's been changing. He'll remember how only a couple years before he might've been able to walk through here without a thought, how there used to be a corner store where there's a coffee shop now; the Baptist church is now a series of apartments. All the lessons he'd learned from other Black people—pay attention to where you are, don't go to X place at night, make sure your hood isn't up when you're walking somewhere, keep your head on a swivel, walk with your hands in your pockets, cross the street when you have to, when you look people in the eye don't do it too long or too short—all of those rules, all of those lessons about being watched or how not to be watched are being shook out by the smug, warm idling engine of a police cruiser in the middle of a place he doesn't recognize anymore.

PART III

CHAPTER 7

The Branch That Came Back

Communities and Neighborhood Transformation

Bunk Johnson on the grounds of Shadows-on-the-Teche. Photo courtesy of Shadows-on-the-Teche Foundation.

*You can't separate what's happening now from historically
what has happened. Because if people can do that kind of evil
and get away with it, what does that tell you about your
power?*

—Dr. Phebe Hayes, retired professor and dean of the University
of Louisiana at Lafayette, *The Acadiana Advocate*, Nov. 4, 2018

I came to New Iberia, Louisiana, back in 2018 through the National Trust for Historic Preservation's Saving Places, an initiative meant to preserve American landmarks that have some type of racial or cultural historical significance. The National Trust brought me there to work with the foundation responsible for managing New Iberia's preserved plantation estate known as Shadows-on-the-Teche. My job was to help the foundation find a new way to tell stories about the Shadows other than the existing ones that mainly focused on the white family who had owned it and often reduced the enslaved Black people to the background, if they appeared anywhere at all. I strutted down to New Iberia full of East Coast swagger. At that point I had lent my pen to essays covering race and contemporary politics in outlets like *Vox*, *Rolling Stone*, *Philadelphia Magazine* and various online blogs. I was feeling confident about my ability to puncture the past and bring everyone forward in facing the past with an honest reckoning. How hard could it be? I remember thinking, This is a Southern plantation still standing in the heart of Louisiana. It just needs to be taken down a notch, right along with anyone who still loves it.

I was, in essence, feeling myself. And it didn't help that even on the Lyft ride from Lafayette Regional Airport to New Iberia, I'd managed to convince my driver, this middle-aged white guy born and raised in the area who worked on a Baton Rouge oil rig with his two sons, to reconsider everything from Kaepernick to rap music.

This, I remember thinking, will be easy.

It's easy to forget that particular era was also about removing racist relics and symbols all over the country. From small towns to big cities, one of the pre-2020 reckonings was focused on taking down statues and plaques, changing public building names and renaming streets that honored the Confederacy. It was around the time that Bree Newsome scurried up a flagpole to snatch the Confederate flag and the persistent dog whistles of white people's disdain that reverberated through it. I came to New Iberia, to the Shadows, with all that; inside my little brown chest beat the swirling hype juice of the burning mansion in *Django Unchained*. I wanted to give Black New Iberians a reparatory fighting chance, and I wanted to rub some kind of moralistic victory in the faces of the white New Iberians, who I'd assumed were all ignorant, violent and resistant.

In the mid- to late 2010s, the notion of vigorously toppling America's racial past seemed front and center in our socio-pop-cultural mindsets. Black people felt like we were on a winning streak; everything from Obama's two-term run to *Black Panther* and *To Pimp a Butterfly* to the NFL getting dragged over the race politics that Kaepernick brought to the forefront seemed to have us poised in an unfamiliar place of cultural promi-nence. I came to New Iberia with this in my chest; when I settled into my little bed-and-breakfast in town, I walked a couple of blocks down to the Shadows and stood in front of the planta-tion's gate. I looked through the Shadows' fenced entrance qui-etly proclaiming some kind of victory; I really saw myself and my little essay project as a liberatory key for this sleepy, South-ern, "backwards-ass" town.

But an outsider, even a Black writer outsider, can't change the fate of generations. Not alone, and certainly not in a five-day trip. Generations past the flagrantly violent days of town terror-ism and hatred, there was still something in the New Iberia air while I was there.

But once I got to New Iberia, it didn't take long for me to realize that I'd probably bitten off more than I could chew. I stepped out of the car and into Louisiana's milkshake-thick summer heat and checked into a quaint bed-and-breakfast, a Southern-style Victorian home far along New Iberia's Main Street. The owners, an older white couple in their late sixties, greeted me warmly, looking at my extra-short shorts and grinning face. For the week that I stayed there, the wife would sit with me at their dining room table after she made breakfast for me and the one or two other guests that happened through. Learning I was an East Coast writer who seemed sensible and smart, she gradually loosened up; by day two she was telling me in conspiratorial whispers how "Muslims, thanks to Obama, are taking over the country, and ruining the good Christian life we built here."

This was what my time in New Iberia was like that week in August 2018; people talked in either open or hushed tones depending on who was around or where we were. They talked one way about race with each other and another way when I was alone with them. They sometimes took liberties with me, letting their tongues slack, like the time the white foundation director casually said "nigger" as she told me and a colleague about a story from the Shadows' past.

As I stepped gingerly around town and conversations with people, my blood thickened between the Southern sugar and the bitter saltiness of New Iberia's climate. The air was quiet and heavy in New Iberia, and on my first day I walked down to New Iberia's main center. In that sense, I'd felt like I was traveling back in time and keeping in step with the town's cultural history; in a series of interviews, Duke anthropology researchers recorded stories from Black Iberia Parish residents about walking into the town. In some of those stories Black folks talked about white people in the parish knocking trees down across the roads into town to make it hard for Black people to get to work, often resulting in them losing their jobs.

And even in 2018 I still occasionally saw Black folks walking on their way to work or to stores along the hot, long roads in and around New Iberia. And it's not like it's a walking town. Still, needing to get around that way made me feel closer not only to Black New Iberia's present, but its past, too.

Over the years, Black New Iberians have carved out their place in the town and its history. They've done it through collaboration with each other and help from the occasional outsiders, but also by firmly pushing the town to confront its legacies by removing the Shadows of the past. And it's mostly worked; they have at least pushed the Iberia Parish area to reconsider story, history, spaces and visibility. But it cost them a lot, and there's no better metaphor for Black New Iberia's struggle for reappropriation than Shadows-on-the-Teche and the stories of the Black people who worked there.

They're stories of floods, fancy parties and Bunk Johnson's teeth.

As the town's main plantation estate, Shadows-on-the-Teche is a multi-acre set of grounds sitting right in the middle of Main Street. The Shadows has always been primarily owned by one family—the Weekses—dating back to the early nineteenth century, when they possessed both the plantation grounds and another location called Grand Côte. But around 1922 the Shadows passed into the hands of William Weeks Hall, the nephew of Harriet Hall, who sold the plantation estate to him for $10,000. Hall was a non-New Iberian, a traveling bachelor who dabbled in music and the arts before settling down at the estate. With a Gatsby-like style, Hall loved to host VIP parties at the Shadows. As a tradition, partiers signed the Shadows' foyer door like it was an oversized guestbook. I saw that door on my visit there, staring at the autographs of Walt Disney, Cecil B. DeMille, Elia Kazan and the director of 1915's *The Birth of a Nation*, D. W. Griffith.

As Hall's VIPs—powerful businessmen, creatives, politicos and the like—wined, dined and congregated together in the lavish parlor room, the Shadows' Black staff ringed them like a Black candelabra, waiting on them hand and foot. While the change in hands coincided with a "gentler" time—Hall was considered a more sociable, friendly and seemingly more benevolent white person than they were used to—a racial hierarchy remained firmly in place.

The Black staff Hall employed at the Shadows were a collection of New Iberians who worked in and around the grounds. In some cases, their families had worked at the Shadows for generations, dating back to Hall's aunt and uncle's long reign. In the Shadows' archival collection, there are photographs and letters that give you a sense of the Black staff's identities and experiences at the plantation. Among them were driver Theophile Viltz, housemaid Louise Bowles and brothers Roy and Ronald, who were landscapers.

In these documents you learn about Louise Bowles's late-night treks to the Shadows from the Black side of New Iberia to fix Hall snacks or a nightcap, and how she was sometimes forced to sit and listen to him speak about his life in New Iberia, his family or his heartbroken love life. When the Great Mississippi River Flood happened in 1927, New Iberia wasn't spared by the angry waters. Despite widespread flooding, the Shadows emerged largely undamaged. And while it's true that Hall provided meals to nearby Iberians and flood refugees, that was only possible because he had Louise Bowles navigate her way to any open stores and then to the Shadows in the midst of the flood to cook the food. Overdue credit is owed.

But if there is any greater proof of the nuance of Hall's social and financial largesse, it is seen in the case of Bunk Johnson's teeth. A New Orleanian by birth, Bunk was born in the early nineteenth century and made his name as a twentieth-century jazz artist who toured domestically and internationally, playing with some of the early jazz greats like Louis Armstrong and Buddy Bolden. Bunk played several instruments—trumpet, cornet, drums, clarinet, saxophone, French horn and slide trombone. When he wasn't touring and performing, he was virtually everything else: a funeral parlor worker in Texas, a dock worker in San Francisco, a cigar maker in the Midwest, and in his home base of New Iberia with his wife and eventual fourteen children, he worked on the grounds at the Shadows.

As with most Black folks of that time, it is difficult to accurately capture Bunk's history. Details about his birth and age are in question, so when it comes to his teeth, the same uncertainty applies: Some people say that he lost his teeth due to poor dental health, while others have said he lost them in the midst of a fight and still others claim it was in an accident. But even if how this brother lost his teeth is up in the air (most stories say it was in some fight in 1931), there's no question that he lost them.

In a letter to his boss Hall, Bunk explained the predicament of his missing teeth (at least two in the front, according to most sources you can find about it) and made a request to be fronted money, a loan so that he could have his teeth replaced. Hall flatly denied the request. Scrupulously itemizing all the times he'd lent Bunk money, Hall wrote: "Your letter is a 'request' for $25. Suppose I had followed your example and 'requested' $35 worth of free work out of the men who have been working to help me out, what would you have thought of me?"

Black jazz musicians took up a collection to get Bunk's teeth repaired so that he could resume his musical career on the road. As always, Black folks found a way.

But finding a way in early twentieth-century New Iberia

wasn't easy for Black folks. Making social progress in community with white people was like pulling teeth; each step forward was often yanked back.

As part of a federal land grant program in 1855, Black New Iberian freed slave Antoine Joseph Carrier was granted twenty-three acres. By 1960, though, white Northerners and Southerners had spent years drilling oil and profiting off Carrier's acreage, not only completely ignoring his ownership, but also never paying the family a cent for the massive profits they reaped from their land.

But then again, perfect conditions have never been afforded to New Iberia. As the town moved through the Jim Crow years and tumbled through the Civil Rights era of the '60s, Black folks kept being subjected to all kinds of indignities in their attempts to be seen as equal citizens.

Injustice in New Iberia wasn't limited to land ownership, either; any and every Black establishment and even any mention of Black progress were up for razing. The 1969 article "The Branch That Came Back" by Sheila Maroney in the NAACP publication *The Crisis* details the 1944 story of eight black professionals who were exploring opening Black trade programs and schools after seeing a shortage of education and vocational opportunities for Black folks post-segregation. This was happening as Blacks were being enlisted in the military and serving overseas during World War II. These professionals, a combination of local doctors, educators and civic leaders, included Eddie L. Dorsey, Howard C. Scoggins, Luins Williams and Ima A. Pierson. They were working with local NAACP leaders Herman Faulk, J. Leo Hardy, Octave Lilly Jr. and Franzella Volter to establish a welding school, a move that angered Mayor William Louard and Sheriff Gilbert Ozenne, who warned this group that if they didn't stop their attempts to better Black New Iberian life they'd be "personally responsible for the consequences."

Not too long after that warning, on a random day in 1944 they were all dragged from their homes, offices, barbershop chairs and family gatherings, taken to the edge of the small Southern town and beaten and forcibly driven out of town by New Iberia's sheriff's office. Their beatings are detailed in Maroney's article. Faulk talks about being "clubbed over the right eye and knocked to the ground" by Ozenne's deputies and then told to "walk out until I was out of the State of Louisiana" with the warning that if he ever returned he'd "be killed." The others had similar accounts. Hardy talks about being "forced to run two miles" along a railroad track as Ozenne's deputies trained guns on him. The cycle and intimidation that they all received was damaging not only individually but collectively; as a result, Black New Iberia was left without medical aid "for several months" due to the doctors being beaten and dragged out of town, and the citizens stalled civically, too, as the NAACP's local branch was temporarily halted.

About twenty-five years later, a similar lashing happened on one of the first days of integrated schooling in Iberia Parish in 1969 at Jeanerette Elementary School, where whites not only lined up to yell and protest their disgust at Blacks attending the school, but a group of white men with rifles tried to scare Black students and families off. Despite that, though, the schoolchildren and their families came back.

And yet, New Iberian Blacks found some small ways forward. On the west side of the town, New Iberian Blacks formed a community, upheld by an invisibly enforced social barrier between them and New Iberian whites. This meant that there were two of nearly everything to accommodate the split groups: Black schools and white schools, Black churches and white churches, Black restaurants and white restaurants, Black cemeteries and white cemeteries.

On my visit there that 2018 summer, it still felt like an invisible axe cut between Black and white people in town. Besides the kindness that seemed to abound everywhere, from the local diner and the town library to gas stations and small stores, Black locals still pulled me aside and whispered some of New Iberia's stories to me. That's in part how I came across their most recent troubles with the sheriff's department, under the tenure of Sheriff Louis Ackal, when a gang of deputies spent years harassing and terrorizing the area's Black New Iberians. While Ackal was sheriff, the department was like a continued mutation that started with Gilbert Ozenne and Deputy Sheriff Gus Walker, who'd also spent years leading law enforcement practices that tortured Black folks in the area. In 2014, during Ackal's second term, Victor White III died while handcuffed in the back of a New Iberia police cruiser; incredibly, the death was ruled a suicide—a ruling that came to be known as the "Houdini Suicide." In 2016 Ackal was indicted by federal prosecutors on several counts of civil rights violations related to other cases. Although acquitted on those charges, Ackal left the New Iberia sheriff's position in 2019, but not before incurring over $6 million in lawsuit payouts. We still don't know how many dark stories from that time were kept in the shadows.

Between the town's library and the Shadows' foundation office, I spent days digging through New Iberia's history, each time finding a new corner of the town I didn't know of before. In between those research sessions, I spent time eating at their diners and restaurants or sitting up in my bed-and-breakfast bedroom, lying across the queen-sized bed, leafing through internet pages trying to understand more and more about the town I was in. One day I walked about two miles in the opposite direction on Main Street and went to the Bayou Landing movie theater and watched *Incredibles 2*, the whole time distracted by the idea that the ground underneath me had bled so much in the past.

My time there sometimes felt lonely; New Iberia managed to

have a vacant feeling even with people around. And reading about history that I wasn't aware of made me feel sad and guilty. I couldn't help but feel as if I should've known the stories of Black New Iberians. As if somehow knowing them would've saved or changed things. I tried to find the slices of Black joy in the archives I poured through. There were early twentieth-century photos of Black children playing outside in their good clothes, Black folks strolling into tiny, bright white churches. I came across pictures of Black children sitting in rows inside of a tiny schoolhouse, each one looking attentive and eager and happy.

Around the same time that those Black professionals were run out of town, Black New Iberians started the Brown Sugar Festival. The Brown Sugar Festival ran from 1950 until the late 1960s as a counter celebration for Black people, by Black people, to the town's discriminatory Louisiana Sugar Cane Festival that barred them from participating. The Brown Sugar Festival was like New Iberia's Odunde; it started in New Iberia's West End, where folks gathered and met each other while eating, listening to music and shopping. It even had its own pageantry; each year a "Queen Brown Sugar" was crowned and carried down the festival promenade, floating above the festivalgoers. Church and volunteer groups made parade floats; Black Boy Scout and Girl Scout troops walked the promenade. Marching bands from local high schools and nearby colleges performed up and down the corridor. Little Black girls decked out in white dresses and gowns were done up for young women's pageants.

The festival petered out around 1966, and then a grassroots push brought it back to life around 2018. Its Black cultural vibrancy has returned with it, too.

In a 2019 interview, Brown Sugar Festival coordinator Anthony Daniels said, "If you want to make New Iberia better as a whole you have to use more of New Iberia." You can see a video on the Brown Sugar Festival Facebook page of Daniels sitting in his car sending out a call to action for Black people to help the festival's post-COVID rebuilding efforts in time for the 2022 Brown Sugar Festival: "If you have any positive inclinations, tag yourself and others."

On top of the Brown Sugar Festival, in the 2010s other groups of Black New Iberians had tagged New Iberia for change, creating a cultural renaissance in the area. As a retired academic after years at the University of Louisiana at Lafayette, New Iberia native Dr. Phebe Hayes formed the Iberian African American Historical Society (IAAHS) in 2018 through a partnership with the Shadows-on-the-Teche nonprofit and the National Trust's Saving Places program. Through IAAHS, Dr. Hayes and a collective of Black Iberia Parish professionals pushed New Iberia forward by making them look backward. While they weren't trying to rewrite New Iberia's history, their archival projects, under the title Silent No More, moved the parish's Black stories and history out of the shadows. As a digital collection, Silent includes old nineteenth- and early twentieth-century photos: Black school-children at the Douglass Institute, a late nineteenth-century ledger with vendor listings and snaps of Raymond Conner, who worked on the Shadows grounds during the Hall era.

And IAAHS's work felt connected to the transformation that the Shadows gradually underwent. What used to be a stately, revered, racially out of touch white mausoleum gradually became a home for garden parties, community events and jazz performances. In the fall of 2018 the Shadows even hosted a one-act play called *Bunk Johnson—Out of the Shadows: A Blues Poem* by a playwright named Ifa Bayeza, who, like me, also comes from Trenton, New Jersey.

According to the play's advertisements, once it was over, attendees would second line to Sliman Theatre, the New Iberian venue just a hop, skip and a jump down Main Street from Shadows-on-the-Teche. I remembered the Sliman; when I had stopped by there during that summer trip a sign on the building mentioned that the theater was originally a grocery store before becoming the Evangeline Theater, a segregated movie house where Black folks had to sit in the balcony before desegregation stubbornly took hold in New Iberia in the '60s.

A post–*Bunk* show second line strutting up to the theater decades later struck me as another clever way for the ghost of Bunk and present-day Black New Iberians to assert their presence in town, reclaiming right along the same spine where the white Louisiana Sugar Cane Festival once prohibited Black people from attending. Right along the same Main Street spine that a likely sodden Louise Bowles traveled to cook and deliver food almost one hundred years earlier during the 1927 Mississippi flood.

Outside of New Iberia's Sliman Theatre, located on Main Street, during my summertime visit to the town. Photo courtesy of Tre Johnson.

I had actually met Dr. Hayes at the Shadows center. She walked in and at one point after being introduced, we found ourselves alone to talk Black person to Black person. Back then, she was already telling me about the work and the vision that she had for Black folks and New Iberia history now that she was retired and had come back home.

At the time, I honestly found it hard to believe her. Not that I thought that she was lying or didn't know what she was talking about. It was just that New Iberia struck me as a town happy to be stuck in the past. For me, New Iberia had sundown-town vibes, especially as a Black outsider. I had spent my time there so far mainly feeling sad and sorry for the Black folks that I ran into, because to me the town felt like I was walking on the set of *Mississippi Burning.*

Every night, it felt like a good idea to be back in my bed-and-breakfast room before it got too dark. New Iberia was a place where I still saw too many Black people having to get where they needed to on foot. A place where, when four different Southern white lady librarians flirtatiously greeted me, I subtracted another five minutes from how long I'd spend looking in the library archives.

A place that, based on the behavior of the white wife who owned the bed-and-breakfast I stayed in, believed that Obama's election was like breaking the final seal on the apocalypse.

That town made me feel like the idea of being a race and culture writer was kinda pointless. So when I sat there listening to Dr. Hayes, I was actually thinking, Ain't no way. Ain't no way this town is going to change. I honestly thought it'd be more convincing if she told me she was about to walk across the street and take down the Shadows mansion brick by brick with her own hands.

About a year later, though, when New Iberia and the Shadows popped into my head, I pulled up the Shadows' website and proceeded down that series of New Iberian rabbit holes. That's how I learned about how the Black New Iberian geniuses went to work rehabbing that place. They didn't settle for a flat history; they found the resources to remake narratives so that when folks talked about New Iberians, they didn't leave out Black stories and experiences. Between IAAHS, the reappropriated Shadows and the reemergence of Brown Sugar, they found cultural homes and experiences that kept Black culture alive and visible to everyone.

It's all impressive given how wild New Iberia's situation remains. This place had decades of racism's decay at its core, so the strength, smarts and ingenuity that went into reimagining it should be celebrated for the genius of their continual execution.

This is especially true since New Iberia still had sentries keeping watch and keeping that climate in place; longtime Iberia Parish Sheriff Louis Ackal ran a terrorizing police force whose practices mirrored the racial violence from 1944. Symbols hang around; the decommissioned Lloyd G. Porter Memorial Stadium was named after the school superintendent who helped run those Black professionals out of town in 1944. The 1940 mural in the town's courthouse, *The Struggle of Man*—described in a *Daily Iberian* article as "darker skinned people hoarding money and gambling under the eye of a lighter skinned man with more traditionally European features"—still hangs over the judge's bench despite letters, petitions and protests from Black townspeople as recently as 2020.

Still, with everything that they've done down there, overall I felt like the Shaq meme: I owe you an apology. I wasn't really familiar with your game.

Dr. Hayes and others set out on a mission to redress New Iberia's history. The mission's not complete, but it's further along every year, and the press interviews, storytelling, documentation, cultural events, local and national grant funding are slowly growing the branch back. And other branches have been growing there, too, to fuck up the cultural ignorance and stagnation that's taken place in South Louisiana.

In 2017 Sofia Coppola's *The Beguiled* debuted in theaters. It was shot at the Destrehan Plantation, located about half an hour from New Orleans and two hours from New Iberia. Coppola was vilified by critics for her decision to erase not only slavery but also the entire presence of Mattie, the only Black character in the novel the film is based on. In interviews Coppola comments that she took Mattie and what her character represented out because she didn't want to be "insulting" trying to tackle slavery, and while that's an artistic choice within her rights, it's a cultural choice that fits a familiar white American pattern of denying and disengaging from cultural truths. And when it comes to America's history during the antebellum period, *The Beguiled* once again beautifies the white people of that time, focusing on their turmoil, while offering at most a casual shrug towards slavery and the humanity of Black people at that time. As a result, Coppola's artistic argument doesn't exist in a vacuum; it fits the wider cultural determination to erase the presence of Black people being enslaved and lightens the level of responsibility that white Americans owned in perpetuating and benefitting from slavery.

So what are the consequences of these actions? Among them are the tendrils of what it means when a kindly white townsperson tells you how "things weren't so bad" and when entire buildings, institutions, placards and muted social boundaries are formed on the basis of spoken and unspoken racism. Yet during that same period Black Louisiana continued to find its voice on the same grounds.

Two years before I'd come to New Iberia, Beyoncé Knowles balanced herself atop a sinking police cruiser on a representation of a flooded New Orleans neighborhood block. She eventually reaches dry land and appears inside an empty plantation mansion. Among the mansion's lush drapes, meticulously preserved furniture, sculpted staircases and vibrant colors, she's joined by Solange, Blue Ivy and a score of other Black women. Together they physically, artistically, passionately, joyously dance in the halls, dressed in an array of clothing, their faces fixed with power and dignity, all as the plantation walls once again reverberate with Black music, although now the cultural, racial and historical power has been flipped.

I thought about how Shadows-on-the-Teche, the "Formation" plantation, Dr. Hayes, Beyoncé, *Bunk Johnson—Out of the Shadows: A Blues Poem* and "Formation" were all in almost simultaneous conversation with each other. So much connected these situations, even in the smallest of coincidences; in New Iberia's Bayou Teche Museum there's a small exhibit noting that the city was the birthplace of Beyoncé's mother, Tina Knowles.

Like Dr. Hayes, Beyoncé came back to her roots with the goal of performing an exorcism. Out went the single story and in came an incantation to unearth the voices, stories and music that have always been there in the shadows.

When I walked New Iberia's Main Street and admired the trees, it felt like a gallows walk. Without even knowing, I could feel those trees had seen so much. I imagined all the Louise Bowleses, Ryan Conners and Bunk Johnsons who worked in the surrounding fields, quietly singing and humming songs as they toiled throughout the day, their voices drifting and disappearing into the night.

In local New Iberia lore, "teche" is believed to come from the Indigenous Chitimacha Tribe's word for "snake." As the story goes, this tribe once engaged in a days-long battle with a teche whose body stretched for more than ten miles. The creature was so long, and the times so long ago, that the battle to defeat this teche took many days, and many of the Chitimacha working together. They used what they had—spears, clubs, bows and arrows—but gradually beat back this creature that had come and imposed itself on their land, their existence and their safety. What was left of the massive carcass gradually decomposed and, in its death, created what is now the Bayou Teche, a source of water, import and export to the area. It doesn't matter if the story is tale or truth; fast-forward to the twenty-first century and that historical battle lives on in New Iberia, where they continue to beat the snake out of town.

CHAPTER 8

Vimeo Killed the Internet Star

Black Folks in the Digital Age

Young Black kid lounging in the National Gallery of Art, Washington, DC, 2019.
Photo courtesy of Tre Johnson.

I believe there is enough for all of us.
—@AmberAbundance

None of our digital spaces were initially built with Black people in mind. Nearly all of them offer the chance to have some harmful experience, as far back as AOL chat rooms and all the way up to today's current social media platforms and media outlets' comment sections. Digital animosity and anonymity have only made these attacks easier and often relentless; Black parents of Gen Z have to have two talks with their kids now: the police and the internet. Bullying, anti-Blackness and bigotry have become the features and not the bugs in every kind of digital room. This had even started before the merging of the digital world and the real one; I remember the afternoon I spent beating mostly white guys at the arcade game *Marvel Super Heroes* in the basement-level student union arcade at the University of Maryland. After I'd spent about three hours beating player after player at the fighting game, a white guy who'd already tried to beat me twice finally got the best of me, jubilantly sneering "get your Black ass back to class" to the cheers of the surrounding guys as I left the arcade.

Not much has changed since the '90s. Today's gaming culture has just as much toxicity baked into it; more even, thanks to cultural incidents like 2014's misogynistic #Gamergate and it's anti-woke follow-up about a decade later in #Gamergate 2.0. In both of those situations, the dominant gamer culture identity—largely male and white—germinated roving bands of harassers that targeted game-world journalists, developers and influencers who they felt were destroying gaming as they knew it. They formed in the twenty-first-century clubs of 4chan, You-Tube, Reddit and Discord, and then took to the digital town squares of Twitter, Facebook and Instagram to dox and issue death and sexual harm threats to anyone and everyone they thought was involved.

And inside the actual gaming worlds, things haven't been much better. The free-roaming early twentieth-century American frontier video game *Red Dead Redemption 2*, released in 2018, featured a hidden side quest where characters could bring a bound Black man to a KKK meeting in the woods, while in its online world people were creating digital gangs that shot, chased and terrorized online gamers with Black avatars.

Even good intentions had disastrous results. Uber-popular battle royale game *Fortnite* boasts five hundred million players worldwide and allows them to play as any number of created and familiar pop-culture characters that they can put into an online arena world and dance, shoot, chase and bop each other. In 2021, *Fortnite* game developer Epic Games wanted to take advantage of their massive platform and use it as a force for good. Through

231

their March Through Time initiative, they re-created a digital version of the United States National Mall, and with it rebroadcasted MLK's seventeen-minute-long "I Have a Dream" speech, complete with associated minigames and an in-game big screen for players to listen to and watch the speech. But *Fortnite* being *Fortnite*, players mostly ignored the importance of the gesture, continuing not only to have dissonant battles between, say, Darth Vader and Pikachu, but also, thanks to the poor timing of a *Wonder Woman* promotion, modifying their avatars with her lasso and taking turns whipping each other in front of the MLK screen.

But if you look inside gaming culture, you'll see something else, too. Inside the same internet that's spawned so much hatred in the gaming world, we've managed to repurpose and create so much safety and joy. As a collection of Black digital identities and voices, we've created platforms, communities and accomplishments that are inherently pushing back on the bullshit. And we've done so through a blend of gaming world know-how and flourishes of Black culture, humor and love—sometimes the biggest missing ingredients in the wider gaming cultural space.

The Blacspiration Podcast, formerly known as *The Unapologetically Black Gaming Podcast*, is what a lot of this looks like at once. As hosts, Cortez Washington and CallMeAzia bring out

Black folks across every identity talking about every kind of game and gaming experience. It's a hilarious space; as one of the hosts, Cortez's deep knowledge as an avid gamer, plus his interest in intersectional identity conversations and just his general Blackness, mean he ends up easily getting his guests to open up and share their thoughts and feelings. Black gamers appear on the podcast by way of their online handles—@Blizzb3ar, @MsPinky313, @TallNQuirky—and when you listen to them, a whole new portal opens up. These folks, a collection of Black women, men and nonbinary folks of all backgrounds and interests and locations, have often steadily carved out their own large followings and cultural positions inside and alongside social gaming giants like Twitch and Facebook, and in some cases become successful enough to leapfrog into gaming and digital content creation full-time.

Go spend time in their corners of the internet. One of my favorite follows I learned about through the podcast is Kandi; her gaming-focused Instagram account @IAm_iKandi_Gaming has almost sixteen thousand followers. Scroll and you'll see Kandi doing everything from Sailor Moon and Cruella de Vil cosplay to merch promotion and convention appearances— in one, she's posing with a Baby Yoda doll. With her full self on display, it's easy to see what makes Kandi's presence so appealing—she's shimmering with realness, sharing full Black geek posts, selfies and peeks into her personal life. She's a live journal of achievements unlocked, giving herself shout outs for partnerships with YouTube and Twitch, announcing upcoming gaming competitions she's participating in and then sharing a post where she's drinking with her friends.

And it's all love; on her Twitch channel with thirty-three thousand followers, she makes it a point, via a rainbow emoji, to say that the space is LGBTQ-friendly.

On *The Unapologetically Black Gaming Podcast* you'll frequently hear the guests talking about pushing back against the entrenched white male gaming culture with communal norms based on love, respect, no bullshit and no hate in their space or presence. *Unapologetically* is a perfect example of Black digital life sitting at the intersection of everything, everywhere, all at once: Black culture, video games, inequality, anime, mental health, racial reckonings, microtransactions and downloadable content. Some of the podcast's best bits are when it's able to incorporate cultural conversations, like talking about how bad Black hairstyles and skin tone options have been in games where you get to create your own player. Or how even in horror video games Black folks don't want to go into the basement of a creepy house.

Cortez's conversational ease and hilarious comments get the people talking. Sure, on *Unapologetic* Black gamers and influencers share their opinions on game design, online gamer communities and familiar headaches in beating certain games. But what makes me stay are the tender, personal takes. Some of the best moments come from when guests talk about how their first video game experiences bring back times with their family or friends, or even moments alone. I get moved by both sets of stories—my video game memories include the childhood times that I sat in my grandparents' bedroom playing *Tetris* with Pop-Pop on the edge of his bed, but also the quiet stretches of my life when I've been single, jobless or just plain alone, and the idea of another world, one where I could definitely win if I kept at it, was the only thing that made me feel competent and safe.

If I was ever on *Unapologetically* I'd talk about some of those times, of seeing Pop-Pop dramatically, comically raise one leg off the bed and lean to the left while he tried to make a rapidly dropping *Tetris* piece flip and fall into place. How he loved level 5, which he always called "the cool level," dragging out the "oo" in "cool" like a string of gum from his mouth. How days after work he'd come into his bedroom and lay across the bed and watch me playing *Tetris* until dinner, humming a song somewhere behind my head.

I'd talk about how some games will always be associated with times and moments in my life. When I moved back to Maryland after teaching high school English in Houston, I couldn't find a job for months. I lived in a second-floor rented place in Laurel, Maryland, and would spend days and nights playing *NBA Live 2004* on this floral-patterned couch that came with the condo, trying to make Ben Gordon and the Bulls champs, ferociously dunking on anyone whenever I played as Vince Carter. I would pass evenings and mornings at the nearby Staples faxing résumés to local school districts and job postings after paying for time on their computers to scroll and look for jobs.

I'd talk about how video games made me everything from lonely to avoidant of my depression, to heroic, to obsessive, to calculating, to happy, to exasperated, to tired, to powerful. How every world I explored in them sometimes felt more alive than the one I was living in.

This podcast is a joy; it's the portable Black Game Boy that I wished I'd had when I felt like I was the only Black kid in the universe battling Koopa Troopas, vampires and giant sewer rats. That I was the only Black kid in college freaked out by my PlayStation 2's controller moving séance-like across the floor during a pivotal scene in *Metal Gear Solid* the first time I played it. Where did a Black kid like me go to find other Black kids glowing with the same unnatural halo of long hours playing *Final Fantasy VII*? It was the same amber-thick geekiness I found myself in as a Black comic book fan—just me alone with my thoughts echoing in nothingness.

Even now, going online can still feel like stepping alone into the wide, cold void of space even though it seems everyone's living on the internet. Trying to find yourself and your way on the internet can feel so disorienting—gaming and gaming spaces were supposed to be places to escape. One of the things that makes video games appealing is their ability to not only transport you elsewhere but also to allow you to feel powerful and competent, even superior in a space.

There was no *The Unapologetically Black Gaming Podcast* then, so long live *The Unapologetically Black Gaming Podcast* now.

And *Unapologetically* isn't the only place where Black gamers can electronically frolic. There are hubs like Jay-Ann Lopez's Black Girls Gamers (BGG), initially a 2015 members-only Facebook group for Black female gamers to have a bunker away from the otherwise (heavily white) boy culture of gaming. For a while, people had to complete a membership questionnaire and even prove that they were a Black woman in order to keep trolls out. But the whole thing caught on major; now, BGG has thousands of followers across not only Facebook but also Twitter, Twitch and Instagram. The BGG IG account is full of bright and bouncy posts featuring Black girl gamers talking about the games they're playing and their thoughts about the latest gaming news, including clips of them playing games and offering hilarious commentary while wearing headsets. Everyone's geek flags fly on it; the comments sections are always civil, humorous, supportive and hype.

More than just a gaming community, though, BGG's also

been at the work of platforming Black women, transforming them into in-community celebrities and turning over the site to their thoughts on not only gaming but anime, food, esports competitions and self-care conversations. BGG is a digital sanctuary, a beautiful glen in the middle of the mean woods of gaming culture where these Black women gamers are flexing joy, building community, spreading love. And on the real, BGG has added even more to the conversation and experience; Lopez has moved the whole thing into a realm where women are powering up through workshops on game development, partnerships with major game sponsors, fanbases that include all kinds of people. She has pushed into the gaming conversations the fact that Black women gamers are forces to be reckoned with, too.

All of this happens away from the toxicity that's been bred by male gamer culture and personalities, some of whom have had their heads go sideways with the fact that the internet has revealed the reality that they aren't the main character and consideration of pop-culture escapism. But back on internet main, if you look, you'll see that there are stories about Black women gamers like QueenArrow and Cuddle_Core who are literally nationally and globally ranked in *Tekken*, a fighting game that's made me so mad in the past that I vowed to quit video games about 5011 times. But as two Black women in their mid- to late-twenties, they're just the sort of identity that angered the types of white male incel-like gamers who instigated #Gamergate and several anti-woke agenda conversations. Despite that culture being present, though, they're winning in every way possible, not just esport *Tekken* tournaments, but endorsement deals, sponsorships and clout. In 2018, Cuddle_Core finished fourth in an international competition with over three hundred players, and in 2021, she finished second in a North American *Tekken* tournament at the age of twenty-six.

These Black women triumphs have forced the world to pay attention, and as a result, people have had to listen to their stories. Cuddle_Core discusses coming from a childhood of gaming, watching and playing with her dad since she was three years old. When she talks about her story, you hear the importance of coming from her hometown of Chicago, of being Black and of being a woman and pushing against cultural and actual competition for space in gaming. She talks about the things you'd expect when it comes to making a mark in gaming; as a Black woman in the competitive arena, she's been judged on everything but her gaming most of the time. But when she talks about how she makes it through the culture, she's got a sense of humor about it and herself—she loves *Tekken* because she loved watching martial arts growing up, and she says she loves "throwing hands," too. When asked about the bullshit super-hit combos of sexism, racism and the question of respect among her peers, she talks about "going numb" and how often she uses breathing exercises or takes naps.

This isn't what you hear from typical gamers who instead talk about the constant need to be the greatest, the endless hours of playing and training and the undercurrent of almost toxic isolation. Cuddle_Core brings joy to herself and to the culture, and it's that very joy that helps her to sustain herself. Care, particularly self-care, and an awareness of herself seem to actually be the ingredients that make her a winner. On social media, you can also see a fuller version of her readily on display; she posts about esports tournaments but will also retweet everything from cosigning positive experiences at local arcades around the country to news from other gaming communities (she's also a member of BGG, of course) and discussions about self-care for competitive gamers. There's even a retweet of a Virginia Woolf quotation: "I am overwhelmed with things I ought to have written about and never found the proper words."

Her words in a Reddit AMA back in 2021 have a similar shine to them. She offers to answer any and all questions about her techniques and expresses a joy in helping others improve. In her introduction she also talks about being a public speaker and about harassment experiences in the gaming community and industry, as well as the importance of diversity in gaming.

Reading it led me down your typical Reddit hole. On another

forum, I came across a post with a *South Park* meme with Cartman saying, "How many times do we have to go over this? You're Black. You can play Tekken." This sparked a string of replies from Black Reddit users sharing their stories of growing up playing fighting games at home or in downtown arcades. I spent an hour reading one Black user after another chime in with the enthusiasm and awareness that a lot of us play these games, too. The comments are hilarious, heartwarming and validating. They just make you feel seen.

It took me being curious about how other people were talking about one of Willow and Jada's *Red Table Talk* episodes to discover The Shade Room (TSR). I started using TSR as a way of gauging how everyone else was reacting to this show. So whenever the Smiths dropped one of their latest bombs, I'd scramble over to TSR and scroll through the comments whenever the account posted the latest *Red Table* clip. A lot of times it felt like sitting in a barbershop or on someone's front stoop, or being in the world's biggest group text talking about what was going down. TSR is darkly genius in this way; their posts purposely don't have a certain sheen to them and can often just look like memes or someone's everyday IG post. That sort of authenticity is what TSR's founder Angie Nwandu has been careful to maintain since she started it up in 2014. With big lettering, lots of hashtags, very short captions and bold images, TSR's got a "jump in, fast" feel to it that deliberately contrasts with "proper" news and journalist outlets, acting more like a digital whisper network. Even now, with almost thirty million followers and over 152,000 posts so far, the platform can still feel like it's letting you in on something that people don't want you to know. After all, if you trusted The Shade Room to give you the "tea" that no one, especially the celebrities responsible or involved, would, then you could also start accepting that maybe its content shared the kinds of truths that they—Democrats, "woke mobs" and "alphabet people"—didn't want you to think or know.

I spent the last couple of years getting turned off by TSR. Their vibes felt increasingly sneaky to me, as they snuck in ridiculous posts like "President Biden approves $30 million to give out crack pipes" in 2022, or later when they went at the administration again for "only" giving out one-time payments of $700 to Maui wildfire victims, when in reality that payment was a part of a suite of support for that crisis. I started noticing that TSR went up to the line of not quite editorializing but often winking at it. For the longest, TSR loved to offer up posts about Magic Johnson's gay son EJ or Dwyane Wade's daughter Zaya, provoking homophobic, slurred responses in the comments section. Black celebrities have occasionally spoken out, too; Summer Walker, LaKeith Stanfield and others have referred to the gossip platform as "cyberbullying," "trashy" and "toxic."

As MSNBC, *BuzzFeed* and media watchdog groups have

pointed out, TSR's approach to popularity meant relying on click- and rage-baiting tactics in order to drive up engagement, often seeming intent on pushing right-wing agendas, possibly due to funding from right-wing sources. I think some of my friends wave much of this off, probably thinking that they're smart enough to not be influenced or lured by the platform's bait-and-switch tactics around politics and sexuality. For me, though, TSR's obvious lack of a moral core made it too hard to ignore; their celebrity gossip and "tea" hasn't been enough for me to pretend that too often the account was indifferent to the harm it was causing because its goal is to keep engaged traffic it can profit from. The harm along the way? Why, that's just unfortunate collateral, and hey, Black folks aren't a monolith.

Left in its wake though are the assortment of more traditional Black media outlets like *The Root*, *TheGrio* and *Atlanta Black Star*, which are now scrambling to be seen as relevant and credible in comparison to something as ridiculous as TSR. On social media, these news media sites are losing the culture war and viewer attention; collectively, they don't even have half as many IG followers as TSR, despite arguably possessing three times the expertise and critical reporting. It's maddening dynamics like this that give me deep pause on outright celebrating TSR's success; the cost is too high, and it's unclear who is actually benefitting besides Nwandu and her stakeholders. If you consider *Black Panther* and Barack Obama as aperture-opening moments in the culture, you can also point to the digital portal that TSR's opened up, which has allowed a deluge of Black podcasters, influencers and gossip sites to populate the social media sphere with everything from questionable takes to questionable backing. The sell to the rest of us has been that these platforms have rightsized the long-standing barriers in traditional media, but that argument is gradually eroding. I stopped going to the digital stoop, because it all feels way too compromised. I scroll on by now, even though I am arguably seeing more Black faces and voices online than ever before.

The argument in favor of the internet and social media is that they have allowed for greater democratization and obliterated a lot of the gatekeeping of information, access and visibility that's held communities like ours back for eons. "Democratization" is an agnostic term in the world of the internet; it's a boon when it comes to BGG and the visibility of Black gamers and our micro community.

But it's also opened hell's mouth for lots of other ridiculousness. Peer inside and you'll see the increasingly toxic gender conversations led by the likes of Kevin Samuels, who made a living off tapping into the insecure, misguided Black male psyche. Samuels's brand was specifically about chastising Black women who he saw as "gold-digging," emasculating and ignorant, his YouTube videos often preying on stereotypes, appearances and gender insecurities. Sometimes he loved to place a tremendous amount of blame at Black women's feat for being undesirable, "unrealistic" and too proud. In one of his virulent videos, he captions his one-on-one debate with a Black single mother in his trademark coarse fashion: "You're FAT, Have 2 Kids. A Man Would Be Settling for YOU!" Wishful thinking would suggest that when he died, these attitudes died with him, but in reality, Samuels's presence was but one head on a cultural hydra that's been hard to cut off.

As Nicole Young detailed in a January 2022 *Elle* essay, there's also the Black Manosphere. She describes the collection that makes up its "fiefdom," writing, "there are many subgroups, rival influencers, competing philosophies, and myriad content creators" that are united under a common manifesto of "a concerted, explicit disdain for Black women." Like #Gamergate, it's an entrenched subculture of men who have toxic idols beyond Samuels and communicate through the familiar internet channels—Reddit, YouTube, etc. In these spaces, the conversations are about value, standards and dominance.

As on *Red Dead*, *Fortnite* and Twitter, for all the big talk these men do, they're often hidden behind anonymous internet handles and identities, which means that they likely move through a variety of spaces in the real and digital world without a lot of us even realizing it. While I don't spend time in those rooms, there have been times that I have realized how much their kind of thinking breathes in the flesh.

Not too long ago, I used the online service Taskrabbit because I needed someone to help me hang a massive wall art piece in my apartment. I've used the service before, and I always scroll through the listings and find Black people to select. The Black man I hired, Kenya, a bookish-looking guy in his early thirties who could have stepped off the pages of *The Boondocks*, came over not too long after.

After we finished hanging the piece, I grabbed us glasses of water to refresh ourselves, and as we stood around in my room, we got to talking. Eventually we started sharing about what we were both seeing in some of the conversations between Black men around us.

"Oh man, truthfully?" he said to me after he chugged from the glass, smacked his lips and looked at me hard. "I feel like so many of our Black brothers don't have anywhere to go or nothing to do, man. They're just so beaten, man. It's sad. I see them on IG and whatnot trying to look important, but that phone go down and . . . I don't know; a lot of these guys are really depressed, I think. And scared."

At a culture writer summit I attended a couple of years ago, a prominent academic writer-scholar shared that she'd been fielding constant death threats and hate speech directed at her via Twitter and other social media platforms. "It's horrible," she told the room, "and the constant comments just wear you down after a while. It's disgusting." At the time, I offered a thoughtless comment in return: "I think we should get off social media," I said, "because these companies don't care." That reflection was far too dismissive of this Black woman's experience. We're so casually unthinking about Black women's dignity, safety and humanity in situations they didn't create or ask for, putting the onus of action and accountability on them, which I can only assume my comment contributed to. "Just leave" might sound like a helpful, practical solution to staying in a place of harm, but why should she and other Black women have to leave the space that so many other people enjoy daily with little to no worries about their safety? Why, at that moment, was I like so many in society, giving these spaces a pass, even with my belief in her experience and my acknowledgment that the companies that own these platforms aren't concerned with her safety?

In some ways, I stand by the sentiment. I don't think these spaces deserve us. I don't know if such a thing is possible, but I wish the answer moving forward was to construct or reconstruct spaces for Black communities, run and owned by Black people. That certainly won't solve everything and is probably far too naïve of an idea.

Is there such a thing as a "safe space" on the internet? Doesn't seem like it. It seems like as Black people, we're forever in search of an ark to carry us to a calmer digital home inside of these massive social media playgrounds. Still, nothing has proven capable of stopping others from encroaching boundaries and intruding by creating fake accounts and resharing our content. The notion of a Black-only space like BlackPlanet that serves as an open forum for Black people to meet, chat and find everything from jobs to partners seems as outdated a notion as Y2K itself. While it thrived for years as one of the biggest and earliest sites for social media engagement, over time founders Omar Wasow and Benjamin Sun couldn't navigate the changing technology or the coming of a behemoth like Facebook.

That still hasn't made it easy to be in the digital media space. In 2016, after it became clear that the enduring Black Lives Matter movement wasn't going to recede anytime soon, reports emerged from *BBC News*, the ACLU, *Wired* and *Mashable* that revealed companies like Geofeedia and Media Sonar were working with various police departments to, among other things, monitor the social media activity of Black protestors and activists. With software and services like Beware, police departments could trace, monitor and act on what Media Sonar referred to as "illegal activity and threats to public safety." Naturally, this included the ability to heavily track hashtags like #BlackLivesMatter, #DontShoot and the litany of other phrases that many of us likely picked up as an extension of the digital activism that's become the norm over the last decade.

People post their hot takes on gender-related topics, debate the appropriateness of Black Philly prom spending, argue about interview dress codes. In 2023, a lot of us were arguing about the decision made by the principal at the Philadelphia High School for Girls, when she denied a graduating senior her diploma onstage in real time because people in the audience cheered for the student as she walked to receive it. The online debate that it sparked was the perfect example of the emotional whiplashing that happens. Everyone—parents, educators, civic leaders, gawkers, students, Girls' High alumni—all chimed in, and fiercely debated what happened for weeks, filling up Facebook posts with comments, tagging fellow alumni, tweeting about it on X and even having an op-ed piece published.

When Black cultural moments happen online, you can feel like you're walking on eggshells. I think about how exhausting some of these were; from 2013 to 2018 arguing about and reacting to Black death felt like a daily tithe. Kobe died in January 2020, a month and a half before the pandemic lockdowns; I heard the news while I was busy writing in a coffee shop that afternoon. By late that night, after reading teary-eyed posts from Black folks, especially men, in utter shock, alongside posts questioning how much he should be mourned, I participated in such a twenty-first-century grieving: I ordered Grubhub, refreshed Facebook to read and chime in on odes and arguments and sat crying on my couch playing as Kobe on *NBA2K*. And then the pandemic happened, and then it seemed like the entire world was watching the horror reel of George Floyd's murder.

If the last decade has given me a gift, it's been the ability to steel myself while navigating the Black opinions and perspectives that have increasingly surfaced. I also think that I became more aware of these videos and understood how to disassociate myself from them a bit more. Because during that same time I became more digitized myself—making appearances on TV, having more and more essays go big, go viral—and saw my name and words appear in texts, emails, classes, social media spaces and posts from friends, family and strangers.

I started walking on eggshells more and more—I wonder if any of you felt the same. I was steadily being forced to navigate so much, too much, just trying to be online—email death threats would pop up in my Gmail from unknown senders, and writing that phrase now just chills me. For about forty-eight hours, someone with a fake Insta account went from post to post calling me homophobic slurs, threatening to come get me. Under my TV clip appearances, accounts would leave nasty comments sprinkled in among the praise and OK critiques (one of my favorites was getting clowned on a social media account that rated your home and office backgrounds when you appeared on TV). And as more and more people became empowered, enthused and enraged enough to share their thoughts about anything and everything online, it suddenly felt trickier to have conversations that were not even necessarily agreeable, but just civic and sensible. And sometimes I wasn't even sure if who I was talking to was really who I was talking to.

And the more I became aware of all of this, the more scared I got. I know I'm not supposed to say that, that I'm really supposed to say that I activated some super-strong Black (male) power, but honestly, I didn't always have that gear in me during that period. I lived alone, especially during that pandemic stretch, when loneliness and isolation seemed to echo like a phone off the hook. Laying in bed restless and buzzed from drinking at home, I'd find myself worrying that one of the internet trolls that were continually popping up in my posts was actually waiting for me somewhere in my apartment. Instead of spending the night fighting those kinds of thoughts, I'd actually take my phone off silent and let the constant social notification dings fill my room just so I would feel like I wasn't alone.

And what can I say? It worked for a bit. It felt better for a bit to take a step back. To check the lights and sweep under the raised loft bed I had then with a broom to make sure no one was there. To pull my cat into bed with me. Ironically, the same platforms and people that had helped put me on as a culture writer now seemed like digital ninjas waiting to shuriken me IRL.

I shrank back for a bit, which I know is exactly how companies and culturists want to scare Black people who talk a certain way, show up a certain way—intimidating us off the internet channels and downplaying us in the algorithms, or pushing us back to posting brunch photos and new Nikes. Better to be agreeing with strangers than fighting them, I guess.

I figured if I didn't always know or trust who I was talking to, maybe I should just say less online.

There are more insidious and far less obvious Black avatars nowadays; people and companies have shape-shifted themselves to fit into almost all of our Black spaces.

We're actively and purposefully being overfed a diet of Black celebrity gossip; fluff entertainment news; intracommunity culture wars around gender, sexuality and relationships; and other largely disposable content. Wading through the internet for credible coverage or commentary about anything lately feels like thankless labor. I'm aware of how often social media and the internet are full of intentional digital detours as well as platforms, personalities and politics that aren't reflective or informative of who we are or what we care about. And even though there's a curation feature on these platforms that's supposed to allow you to have control over what you see, IG, Twitter/X and Facebook still populate feeds with posts and accounts you haven't asked to see. This is mainly because these apps are ultimately cajoling you into staying enraged and engaged, and one of the ways to do that is making sure they keep you on your heels by sliding you new content, voices and images.

If these avenues are the collective future, what's it mean that some of our biggest online footprints right now are pop-culture memes and search engine optimization–geared hot takes like "Twenty-Five White People That Can Get the Cookout Invite"? There's room for fun and silliness, but the Black room's getting crowded with a lot of this. The proliferation of podcasters pushing poison are profiting from poor politics.

So-called influencers feel much more like infiltrators, snaking onto our social media timelines, nesting themselves in, scouring for any kind of content to boost engagement. They've created an angry algorithm that's been great for retweets, reposts and responses but has done little to actually advance our collective knowledge, freedom or sense of justice. They've also shoehorned themselves into journalism and culture spaces under the guise of "democratizing" the industry, but too often the effect has been to undermine many skilled, experienced, thoughtful Black voices.

BLM's digital justice era created a series of online personalities, including a cluster of people who saw an opportunity to use the movement and all the various deaths associated with it to become activist avatars. What ensued was a series of online skirmishes rallying behind familiar war cries calling for white people to "Do the work!" or stop "Putting the labor of learning on Black and marginalized people!"

While these are the right messages, they have such a copy-and-paste lack of originality to them when they appear across accounts—particularly when they're repeated by non-Black social media personalities—that they smack of falseness. While it's important to reinforce a lot of these messages, they most often end up feeling like the trite social-justice sloganeering that's become a part of our culture and has stood in for uncomfortable, practiced activism out in the real world. These reels and posts, sprinkled with the folky "y'all," will inevitably name-check *Parable of the Sower* and come with the requisite hashtags—#SupportBlack___. The à la carte pulls from culture activists like adrienne maree brown, Ijeoma Oluo and Tarana Burke are a testament to these women's brilliance, but they've also translated into the sort of ephemeral aping that other people pick up as activists du jour.

Still, especially between 2016 and the Summer of Racial Reckoning in 2020, you could almost predict when the flood of reels, posts and diatribes unpacking how clueless people are would come, watch the doors fly open at the White Churches of Praying for the Oppressed, its members holding up the latest anti-racist books like Bibles, eyes tight with tears, faces flushed with anger. They are digital televangelists, imploring you and themselves to do better, be better, and all you need to do is like, comment, validate—and click on their Linktree to purchase branded sweatshirts, T-shirts, mugs and jammies. You can find the link under #BreonnaTaylor.

Occasionally, I was invited into these cultural churches. Like many Black writers and voices, I experienced that four-year period as something like a rock tour; I was appearing in every small-room and big-room conversation imaginable, asked to share my thoughts on race, Black life, white complicity and moving forward. I spoke at Ivies, colleges, universities, K–12 schools, online book clubs, in-person book clubs, panels, guest talks, keynotes, coffees, drinks. I saw my face and my name tagged in more places than graffiti, and during some online talks I felt myself zoom out and wonder if I wasn't living in some sort of cultural thinking purgatory.

My self wasn't myself and my identity wasn't my identity for a while; instead, I was a digital projection and vessel for scores of others to interact with. I started getting published back in 2016, when I wrote about Prince's death for *Philly Mag*, and spent the next couple of years being published and making appearances about Black cultural and political topics. I both felt like and was seen as an adept, sharp Black cultural writer; between *Rolling Stone* and CNN, *Slate* and *CBS Mornings*, I was writing and commenting on a range of topics, including Aretha Franklin's death, Childish Gambino's "This Is America," Netflix's *Luke Cage* series, Michael Jackson's legacy and Beyoncé's *Homecoming*. Those were good pre-pandemic years, when sleek black car services would scoop me up from Philly to take me to NYC studios, and I'd sit in greenrooms next to everyone from

Kierna Mayo to Phil Knight. My image and my name appeared and reappeared all over the internet, and I hustled my ass writing, lecturing and commentating literally all over the country.

And then 2020 happened. And when it did, with exasperation, I ironically found myself back where I started—writing about Black pain. I was writing at the intersection of the pandemic and the racial turmoil, and with everyone cooped up and paying attention to every inch of life that happened, the things that I wrote about got to be seen by a lot more people. And soon enough, like a lot of other Black folks, I started getting inundated with requests to speak online at private schools, colleges and universities, nonprofit professional development talks, workshops and online classes. Just like a couple of years before, I was often being framed or introduced as an "activist"—a title that I never called myself, but one that I think served the purposes of the people who extended these invitations to speak. It gave them a lot of credit because I had all the right credentials—I'd been on TV, spoken at big-name schools, had big-name bylines and, most importantly, I was a palatable, lighter-skinned Black guy who was now writing about race during the latest stretch when people needed to bring Black voices in. Saying yes to these digital town halls and podiums felt dutiful, even if I often found the inevitable question of "How do we fix this?"—meaning anything from racism to society to capitalism—to be both unfair to the lone Black voice in these settings and exhausting, as I had to have a pithy answer that felt graspable and satisfying.

The year 2020 felt like my own Year of the Avatar; I was a Black Max Headroom talking head in all these places. And sometimes I felt self-conscious because I wasn't trying to be seen as either an activist or an opportunist posing as an activist in order to gain money or access. Not that the latter was often even an issue; some places never paid me anything or would hilariously pay me in gift certificates to spend with their organization.

Being a thought leader, activist or policy recommender was never the plan for me, but it was foisted on me thanks to the franticness of that time and what people projected that I could give them in the span of forty-five minutes to an hour. At the height of these talks from June to October in 2020, I was doing upwards of four or five a week, on top of TV appearances, my job and continuing to write. That sort of repetition became mentally and emotionally numbing; constantly being "on," precise, intelligible and engaging was its own digital performance. Add to that the climbing social media followers, commenters and DMs that I felt obliged to respond to and engage with, and it's no wonder that as bountiful as that time was, I was also dealing with not only feeling hollow, but maybe looking it more, too.

And then, like some kind of fever dream, by 2021 it was like none of this, none of the blood, the talks, the books, the "Thinking of you, no need to respond"—it was like none of it, none of us ever happened. Collectively, it seemed to vanish into nothing, not so much replaced by something else as met with an imperceptible shrug as people moved on. Even the social media trolls with their death threats got bored with me! If 2014 and 2024 were #Gamergate years, then 2016 to 2020 should be called the #Racegate or #Blackgate years. Whatever you want to call it, the love and care for and visibility of Black experiences started disappearing online bit by bit.

That should be something of a collective fear.

What if we were doing all this work only to end up being erased years down the line?

N. K. Jemisin's blog anxiously pondered where we, as Black people, are in the future. As she ticks through pop-culture sci-fi stories like *The Jetsons*, *Star Wars* and *Tron: Legacy*, each time she catches the ways Black people are either not present or eliminated in these entries. A 2022 survey by Morning Consult found that 5 percent of Gen Z sees "influencer" as a viable, aspirational career option, while a UK study of the influencer economy that same year found that there's a 35 percent pay gap between Black and white influencers. The false optics of the vocation are driving a generation to chase fool's gold at any cost. We may be watching the internet eat Black life through capitalism. People are chasing a ghost of a chance to make a living off the internet, and the internet? It laughs.

We won't matter if we ultimately just become digital ghosts.

Continuing to barter our dignity, sanity and vanity to the internet won't age well for either us as individuals or our collective culture. Even if abandoning it entirely now feels impossible, we should consider rejecting the digital world a bit more and striking a better balance for our futures, because the answer to a better world relies on figuring out the ways to live in both the digital one and the real one. We have to prepare and build towards the other side of tomorrow so we don't allow ourselves to become erased in society's pursuit to move forward.

CHAPTER 9

The Imagined World

The Future Black World

While in Savannah, GA, for a Jack Jones Writing Fellowship in 2019, I met a local who talked to me about his hopes and dreams for the future. Photo courtesy of Tre Johnson.

I don't like movies when they don't have no niggas in it. I went to see Logan's Run, *right? They have a movie in the future called* Logan's Run. *Ain't no niggas in it. I said, Well, white folks ain't planning for us to be here! That's why we gotta make movies.*

—Richard Pryor, *Bicentennial Nigger*

You remember my nephew? The one who makes figurines from pipe cleaners, memorizes movie facts and re-creates entire Michael Jackson routines all while getting harassed at school?

There are so many times that I try to imagine what a better, kinder world would look like for him and his older sister.

My niece is the family's next big genius. When a lot of other kids spent the pandemic playing video games, suffering through learning loss, tossing themselves into Lord knows what online, she started teaching herself how to speak and write Japanese by reading language books. She's got notebooks full of Japanese words and phrases in her own handwriting. One day, as I'm babysitting her while my sis and nephew are on a school field trip together, we're driving around Trenton, and she tells me that when she grows up she wants to be a forensic detective.

When I ask her why, she quickly tells me, "Because I want to give closure to family members who lost loved ones." Part of what I hear is that my niece wants a better, kinder world than the one she sees.

Which means that I want a better, kinder world for my niece.

My sister is a single mom, and between the local NJ public school district her kids attend giving her headaches about how they're treating my nephew and the countless emergencies that come up for my niece because of lingering mysterious stomach issues, my sister has to move with the kind of speed and strength of a comic book hero. This means that it's also hard to find the kind of jobs that will let her be the responsive, caring and attentive mother she prides herself on being despite what it costs her in return. The rest of us help how and when we can, but it hurts not to be able to do enough to ease her burdens.

Which means that I'm trying to imagine a better, kinder world for my sister.

My mom has been retired for several years now, and she and my stepdad want to travel and see the world as much as possible. Like a lot of Black folks, they love a cruise and try to take cruise trips a couple times a year. Bermuda, the Dominican Republic, the Bahamas, Mexico and parts of Europe. I have so many memories of how hard my mom worked when I was a kid and the number of times that she had to put up with bullshit to keep a job. And even now when she's fully retired, her bones and spirit are stretched trying to do what she can for my sister, niece and nephew. Sometimes when we talk on the phone, she sounds so tired. We stress about the various futures for our family.

Which means that I'm trying to imagine a better, kinder world for my mom.

A lot of the time, I drive back to Philadelphia crying in my car after seeing everybody. I want to cuss out everyone and everything that's making things so hard for my family, and at the heart of it, I am mad and scared because I often feel too helpless to change anything for them.

Which means that I'm trying to imagine a better, kinder world for my family.

And imagining means that I'm still trying to find the deeper answers that I could never utter on all those Zoom calls, workshop talks and college lectures.

I know there's a better world somewhere out there, even if it's only imagined. One that doesn't require so many of us to think we have to go it alone, where every existing system doesn't seem like it's working around the clock to destroy us. I'm trying to think of a world where our story isn't about bootstrapping it or shaming other folks because they aren't bootstrapping it like we did or have to, a world where collaboration and not competition is the first vibe we respond with.

I want to imagine and create a different world for my family. I want to find what it would take to create the Black kingdom that lives in my head where Black children and their families can create the futures they want.

I believe that somewhere right beyond our reach is an imagined world where Black people's abundance can stretch further than it already has. And to get there, we'll need to pull from every possible resource to illuminate the path. Time seems to both grow short and exist within a seemingly unbreakable loop. Just as we were brought here, Black Americans are once again living inside of a society and societal mindset that engineers itself against our political and economic mobilities. Our housing access and options continue to shrink. Cities are becoming less habitable for us culturally, socially and politically—I'm not sure there's a "Chocolate City" anymore. In schools and companies, every resource from curricula to culture leaders are disappearing. Vestiges of old methods of collective power like unions are routinely challenged and dismantled. And the idea of policing has subtly and not so subtly been deemed the solution to America's "Black problem."

We already have the answers to what it would take to have a better, kinder world around us, we just need collective consistency to make it happen. And when you look at the history, you see a metaphorical and literal set of resources that might be the keys to move us forward, by both reexamining our mental, cultural and societal mindsets and adding measures of healing and reflection. And perhaps now more than ever, we need to revisit the perspectives of the Black creative, who is often challenging us to recognize the opportunity to make the imagined world a real one.

Someone dropped it into the group text with a line—"Have y'all seen this?"—followed by a link. I clicked on it and spent several minutes watching a looping series of images called *White People Won't Save You*, Terence Nance's endless series of film clips pulled from *The Last Samurai*, *Avatar*, *The Help*, *To Kill a Mockingbird*, *Hidden Figures*, *Blood Diamond*, *Glory*, *Lincoln*, *Green Book* and loads more. The whole time a choir sings in the background: "White people won't save you . . . white people won't save you . . . white people won't save you." Their voices are in a high register; they sound angelic, prophetic, mocking, sage-like and foreboding. Over time, the steady streams of footage—of white people adopting, indoctrinating, occupying, hiring, whipping, fighting alongside, representing, charming, hugging, parenting, coupling, filming, shooting, walking and running with an array of Black characters, scenes and situations—start to meet and work in synchronicity with the choir. The chant gradually becomes something more; as you sink deeper into the scenes, hearing "white people won't save you" over and over again, you start understanding that the phrase has multiple meanings—that despite their best efforts and intentions, that in spite of what they might say otherwise, that no matter what you might want or ask for, or how much it might require white people's efforts, at the end of the day, they won't save us.

Cultural deprogramming is something of a thing for Nance. I got introduced to him by an HBO representative who sent me a preview of his series *Random Acts of Flyness*, which premiered in 2018. The first episode's overall effect represented an attempt to help viewers deprogram ourselves from a series of societal racial codes and norms. The opening scene begins with a chase, as a young Black man is pursued by a police officer through a snowy tenement area, and ends with flight. In another segment, a Black woman poses as a stand-in for the grim reaper and ushers a small group of Black children towards the notion of inevitable Black death. In one of the more surprising twists, *Mad Men* star Jon Hamm appears in a brief skit talking about reimagining whiteness. The show's format—jarring, fast-cut scenes and images—can often feel like being in *A Clockwork Orange* and having your thoughts forcibly reconditioned.

After I watched it on my couch, I sat in a stupor. What was that? I thought to myself, completely engrossed in what I had just seen. My brain felt jaggedly cleaved down the middle and messily half reassembled. I watched it again, hoping to catch something more straightforward that I had missed, especially since I was set to interview Nance onstage for the New York Television Festival. But not much about any of my first impressions changed. I was broken, or, better put, I was remade by what I saw.

Random Acts was one of those things that might've slipped under most people's radar when it was released; it wasn't the sort of comfortable pop-culture capture that most people would watch. It often felt more like a constant exercise in disorientation; Nance's project constantly shifted the social ground under your feet, and each episode required you to reexamine any number of closely held beliefs. Just like the looping series of images in *White People Won't Save You*, *Random Acts of Flyness* wasn't asking a question so much as asserting a belief: This world ain't it; there's a better one out there.

Both *Won't Save* and *Random Acts* were the perfect opposites of something like Mark Anthony Green's 2016 short film *Fair Use Vol. 1 (All This Trouble)*, a curation of images about the ongoing exploitation and disposability of Black everything—people, culture, contributions, pain, joy—at the hands of an uncaring, parasitic America. *Fair Use* does this by cycling through clips of news, pop culture and protests involving Black Americans. Where *White People Won't Save You*'s mantra is its name, *Fair Use*'s mantra is a looping interview clip of James Brown singing "Living in America." The former is looking to break you out of a spell that the latter is reminding you has been cast.

But what if there's another way? Consider that the imagineers and the healers are the keys to unlocking an imagined world where we as Black people might be able to live far more abundantly. When I watch and share *Fair Use*, it's because I'm mainly trying to remind myself and other Black folks how much this country doesn't deserve us, our genius, our pain, our hopes and dreams, our children, our bodies, our thoughts.

I showed *Fair Use* with some other clips to a closed-door meeting of Black public-sector leaders convened together in Chicago. As the dinner keynote speaker, I was there to present an evening lecture on storytelling. I played *Fair Use* alongside work by Arthur Jafa and archival footage of a forum discussion of middle-class Black folks who'd relocated to LA speaking about the fear they had of "ghetto" Blacks moving there and changing things. I told this crowd that what I wanted to do was remind us that we have more than one story to tell, more than one world inside of us, and that often telling the story that satisfies other people will inevitably cause us some cultural harm; we'll deny the worlds that we exist in and stay tethered to ones that neither fully see nor serve us.

These three pieces—*White People Won't Save You*, *Random Acts of Flyness* and *Fair Use*—should be part of a curriculum around the boundaries we could be stretching or breaking in order to widen the Black world we live in. They're instructive in exploring what else can and must be true for us in our current reality. There are so many things we've been told and learned to hold on to so tightly—in that Chicago room, for example, some of the Black folks balked at the images and quotes I shared, feeling that sights and stories of us twerking, rapping, dancing and hanging in shopping mall parking lots late at night as souped-up cars spin in circles were nothing more than the stereotypical shit we're always seeing Black folks do. But part of us collectively being free as Black people involves reconciling our desire to police both ourselves and other people.

Which is why letting go is a critical part of reimagining what the future world can look like.

At the onset of the COVID-19 pandemic in March 2020, restaurateur Tunde Wey took to Instagram and released a multipart series of posts with the fiery all-caps headline "DON'T BAIL OUT THE RESTAURANT INDUSTRY." In these posts, Wey talks about "frontline communities"—comprising various types of marginalized Black and brown, immigrant and non-American populations situated across the globe. In the context of potential precipitous change and disruption due to the pandemic, Wey reminded us that the elite were already enjoying the excesses of convenience.

We live in a world where anything you desire can probably be delivered to your door in a matter of hours. Food, toys, electronics, clothes, even other people can be picked, purchased or swiped to deliver any measure of immediate or almost immediate gratification. And the cost of that, the ease of transaction—for the impulse Amazon delivery, the lazy-night DoorDash order, the Gopuff grab and the rideshare downtown—is one of human labor. And a lot of that cost is our own people running around on e-bikes and e-scooters, their own car or a leased Tesla, in the interest of performing for our luxury.

They package and wrap things with brutal speed, work endless shifts with little to no breaks, answer to wild turnaround times on orders and get graded with stars and delivery times. I think about my cousin talking about working shifts at an Amazon warehouse not far from Trenton, how he'd be working eight- or ten-hour shifts with fifteen-minute breaks. I think about the tell-alls about warehouse work conditions where people are pissing in water bottles and soda cans because floor managers aren't giving them break time and are deciding who to keep based on output and package assembly.

I think about the times that I sit looking at a screen feeling annoyed because a delivery order might be forty-five or fifty-five minutes when I want it to be sooner. Or when the Lyft ride is a ten-minute wait and maybe five dollars more than I think it's worth. How the convenience economy masks that every time I want something faster, someone human, someone who more often than not probably looks like us, needs to move faster along the assembly line.

Wey goes on to say, "Spotify and Netflix distract our souls . . . Uber Eats, Instacart and Amazon deliver to our bodies," illustrating the notion that even the slightest tweak to our entitled existence leads us to only the most apocalyptic nightmare scenarios. "The end will not come as predicted by our silver screen imagination—this apocalypse won't feature roaming hordes of bandits stealing for pleasure and necessity, Tupac, California Love style," Wey writes. "So forget fantasies of close combat in decayed buildings choreographed to the lowing of wild dogs."

I reread Wey's IG posts again after the pandemic's restrictions were lifted and started seeing them as a call for greater societal intimacy and connection. I started thinking about how an inability to see everyone's humanity on a day-to-day basis might be holding all of us back from seeing everyone's fullest potential. I thought, too, about how often we rely on each other for things we need without thinking about the costs of those needs—that goes back to Wey's anger about how much we take working-class Black and brown folks for granted. What if we were in better community and connection? What if we could see each other's worth? What more could we do together?

Wouldn't it be genius to band together and turn this whole way of thinking and seeing each other on its head?

Wouldn't we all benefit from a better, kinder world?

I believe that there's a world where all these things can exist—our desire to have beautiful, safe places to call home; to have an unbroken lineage of excellence as well as the freedom to be mundane; to speak, live art and love without the compromise of anti-Blackness, inferiority or commodity; to be able to breathe, I mean really breathe, without wondering which breath will be your last and without wondering when you'll get fired, or evicted, or shot, or followed, or surveilled. In the imagined world that I see, Black folks don't have to contend with anyone but ourselves. It's perhaps the most militant and Garveyesque thing about my personality, which is ironic given that Garvey is a question mark around the murder of one of my relatives. It's not that I hate the presence of anyone and everyone else who's not Black; it's that I hate the dynamic of fitting ourselves and our stories and our needs and our bodies into the currently established America alongside everyone else. We expend so much energy showcasing and arguing for the right and beauty of being Black that I can't help but wonder: What if, in an imagined world, we didn't have to worry about this and could really, truly contend with ourselves?

In essence, we need to think about developing a new kind of home where our genius can thrive.

There's been other writing about rehoming ourselves as a community. In 2015 *The Bitter Southerner* published Lolis Eric Elie's "Why We Came Home," an essay that unspools a decade's worth of reflections about what and why it's been important to return to the once-sunken city of New Orleans. Despite so many Black New Orleanians having to leave, so many were also drawn back to NOLA, desiring to reclaim a home that was unfairly taken from them. So much of the why circulates around battling the lopsided capitalism that was just as abhorrent as the storm.

Through a series of sometimes painful, sometimes humorous stand-alone sentiments presented as a list, each one starting with "Some of us," Elie references everything from insurance payouts (or lack thereof) to feeling at home elsewhere ("Have you ever been to Kalamazoo?") and faith ("For the poor will never cease out of the land"). But it serves as a calling and a reminder of the undeniable, magnetic pull of wanting and having a place to call home. We want a home at any cost because we deserve one and we love a home with the people we love (and maybe some we don't love so much) around us. And Elie's piece is a beautiful siren song to come back home that probably hits for a lot of us.

Journalist Charles M. Blow's 2021 *The Devil You Know* is a Black manifesto making the case for Black folks to move en masse to the South to consolidate Black political power, tip the scales in our favor and change the outcomes for Black lives.

But parts of both the ideas of moving South and consolidating Black political power as a sort of reverse Great Migration feel like grand sentiments and plans. I think there's more; there are answers here sitting in the middle of both of these pieces. And I think if we can try doing the following, we might be able to create and love even more Black geniuses in our midst.

One major way to explore fostering Black genius is through urban and nonurban communes. Pockets of intentional community where we share resources, buffer ourselves from outsiders and antagonists and have broader canvases to explore ourselves and be in community with birth, chosen and blended families, might be the way to go. In urban settings, this would mean figuring out ways to coordinate owning large blocks of housing and potentially being OK with the idea of shared, rather than singular ownership, as well as acknowledging the fact that not everyone may have the financial means to contribute towards ownership to the same degree. I'm picturing areas where a lot of the things we've already talked about would be way more possible: For example, childless people who wanted to have children but didn't or couldn't could play parental roles and develop meaningful relationships with children. The primary birth and adopted parents would have nearby support eager to be a part of a family unit. With more people in the mix, children could be cared for more, loved on more, mentored and supported more. Families wouldn't be stuck with the stresses of day care or home care, and maybe even schooling, in the commune model.

A commune would be great for creatives and gig economy people, too, those in professions that are often high on mental and bodily demands and short on income, self-care and support. For people who want to expand the boundaries of love, friendship and partnership, too, communes afford opportunities to make choices in community with others and minimize some of the additional risks of trying and discovering things on your own.

Can you see it? I can. Imagine a commune being like a massive living room with all your favorite people in it. Michael Twitty's in a kitchen cooking alongside Black children and young adults, showing them the recipes from our enslaved ancestors, grounding them in the techniques, the patience, the ingredients, the stories, the flavors. I first came across Twitty through his 2019 essay "Dear Disgruntled White Plantation Visitors, Sit Down," where he reads some white visitors who expressed dismay at the lack of slave reenactment authenticity on a plantation tour. Twitty has been perfecting the cooking practices of "colonial and Antebellum ancestors," painstakingly recapturing a Black diaspora of West African nations in former slaveholding states and on the stained grounds of plantations, and discovering their methods, meals and motivation around food.

For Twitty, food is his way of tracing his family's lineage to freedom. In the imagined world, we'd have a cadre of Twittys learning, sharing and apprenticing with each other about the importance of being fed through culture, history and identity.

Maybe in someone else's living room, Christopher Priest is listening to a conversation between some drill rappers and Lorraine O'Grady, drawing ideas and inspirations from each other. Or maybe just talking about life. These could be places and homes to teach and dialogue with each other about the sorts of cultural curricula that not all of us are exposed to. Not everyone's read *All About Love* or any number of Octavia Butler's books, or is aware of the speeches that my ancestor James Eason gave—or thought about the ways to put them all together.

What if communes meant we relied on digital communities and marketplaces less? What if we found that the best, richest connections are the ones we are able to foster right here, right now?

To have someone ease some of the burdens would free us up to do so much more. A commune could allow us to take more time and more risks. With shared resources and living, I think we could introduce more and longer periods of rest, even giving each other creative periods like sabbaticals.

I want a world where our people aren't bound by limited time to grieve. I want us afforded the time, care, love and space to grieve as long as possible for whomever we've lost. And because grief requires rest, I want a world where people take a sabbatical whenever they need it.

Right now, retreats, sabbaticals, rest periods for things like grief, are most abundantly available to the well-resourced and connected—many of us can't even conceive of allowing ourselves the proper rest and reflection periods we need. But I want everyone to have access to rest and the time and space to reflect—from wage workers to white collar. This is not only possible but vital.

The commune experience would also be a source of continual joy.

What if every day after school and work there was a commune flash mob of kids, teens and adults? What if every night felt like BlackStar as we gathered and watched some dope new shit together? What if every Sunday was Odunde and we rotated communes to have open-air marketplaces where we fed, entertained and chatted with each other?

What would that free us up to do? To believe? To try? What if we found we'd been holding so much back, so much inside, because we were first and foremost trying to survive? I do not want to be in competition with my people, because competition, I have found, requires us to believe that in order for one of us to succeed, one of us must lose something.

I'm saying to you, what if we were in a race to see how much more we could give each other?

This shouldn't be surprising. At this point, we've looked at how often we've been able to develop, define and explore genius by being in community with other people. *All-Negro Comics*, Milestone Comics, the allure of Wakanda, New Iberia's cultural reclamation, Fried Shrimp Wednesdays and even the Philly and Black city urban biker and racing clubs all speak to the power of finding your people, building with your people, sharing with your people and making something beautiful together. Those situations have been about sharing resources, redefining what's possible together instead of in isolation and lessening the burden and the labor of doing it alone. These creative and cultural commutes are blueprints for how we should continue to aspire to build labs of Black genius while taking care of each other.

What's at stake? I think of Athena Dixon's *The Loneliness Files* and its intimate meditation on the tenderness that comes with loneliness, isolation and individualism. Even though it was written during the pandemic, many of her reflections, observations and obsessions around community, connection and touch are just as relevant apart from that time, in a world where money, grind culture, housing and love are all most often treated like individual pursuits. I think about the energy she and others of us could have in a consistent, connected community, and how much more we'd create, how much less stress we'd have, how much more love there'd be around us. Loneliness and isolation may have been key pandemic features, but they can also be their own personal pandemic. And in the vastness of loneliness, it can be hard to figure out life in a world that can feel so cold and alienating.

My imagined world is essentially a borderless world. That's both literal and metaphorical; I don't want us to have to establish new plateaus and ventures and identities against the grain of oppression but rather to move towards the flow and in the forward vein of love.

In June 2020, I wrote an essay for *The Washington Post* titled "When Black People Are in Pain, White People Join Book Clubs." The essay was inspired in part from getting a Facebook notification that some old white friends of mine had started a Facebook group event for them to read "anti-racist books" together.

It made me so angry; these were friends I knew saw each other all the time over dinners, summer trips and drinks. Friends who I knew had spent years working in Black communities and schools, who talked about the ways schools and districts were failing kids—and had worked in them. Who had spent intimate time with me and other Black people, and had, I thought, routinely heard the stories, the frustrations, the hurts that we'd all talked about. Looking to start a book club felt, at that time, incredibly passive. They might as well have done nothing. While my white book club friends were figuring out scheduling, book selections, who would host and what the rotation would be, I was on phone calls and group texts talking about protection protocols. I marched right down the three flights of my apartment building and up Christian Street for about six blocks, hooked a left on Broad Street and joined a throng of protestors that were like a river of salmon going against the cultural tide of things like sitting at home, making up book clubs, writing sanctimonious posts on social media or resharing with the all-caps "THIS." I mean, Floyd had the air leaked out of his life like a balloon thanks to that man's knee on his neck. We all watched it from online, but a book club felt like a way some people chose to stay away from understanding what racial violence felt like for them, which made me think they actually didn't feel anything.

I watched and let myself feel in much the same way that imagining Breonna Taylor's death was like a horror reel of feeling.

Their deaths felt like all the things that I had to learn as a child to tell myself not to be scared about—the world, and that the world had boogeymen all around you that no one else seemed aware of. Boogeymen that could get you on the street or wait until you were in bed and slide under your door, or pop out of your closet or, in the middle of a random morning, beat down your door and take your life. This is, of course, taking a lot from a notification, but I'm saying that if there were fifty actions that first come to mind in light of these things, a book club—either participating in one or starting one—wouldn't even be 51, 68, 109 on the list.

That Facebook notification about starting an anti-racist book club struck me as just so lazy, feckless and just completely out of touch. It just felt like a performance, honestly, because I knew that, like most book clubs, it would either peter out in meeting or in conversation. It was only a matter of time before it would devolve into tipsy get-togethers, where talking about the latest or most important book would be an inconvenience. When they'd get together as friends, topics like kids, work, partners, house repairs, family issues, reality shows would feel way less stressful and mentally draining to talk about on a Wednesday night over malbec and cheese plates.

I was so 2020; I of course ranted about my anti–book club feelings on Facebook and felt like that was that. Super cathartic, hot-headed stuff in that moment.

But it was another Black writer, Cynthia Greenlee, who told me what to do with that anger. "Sounds like something you should pitch an essay on," was the comment she left on my emotional Facebook post. That essay, written when we were all bottled up inside our homes, went viral, and by the end of the week all my follower counts across every social media platform I was on had grown exponentially. I got tagged constantly, DM'ed incessantly, and received invitations galore. Before I knew it, one of those invitations turned into a trip to Martha's Vineyard, courtesy of a Hollywood VIP.

It was Labor Day weekend 2020, and my first time on the island, a place that before then I'd only associated with boat shoes, rich white people, bougie Black people and the sort of stuffy Americana elitism that somehow still felt charming. On the ferryboat to the island, while I watched the waves from the outdoor deck, I tried to imagine how to act once I got with the people I'd be spending time with. I honestly felt so confused about what I thought about being around strangers for the first time in months; like most people at that point during the pandemic, I hadn't meaningfully spent time around strangers for a while. I only felt numbness staring out from the deck.

But more than anything else, as I touched down and spent the weekend there, I found myself thinking more and more about what a Black world could look like back on the mainland. How the space of being away gave me the breath to think and imagine, which made me realize how hard it was to breathe and imagine living in the city back on the mainland. I thought, and still think about, what little support there is to grieve and take sabbaticals if you're most of us. There's so little room to grieve and get away. There are a lot of things that I could say about how magical that time on the Vineyard was, but the biggest magic was having the time to imagine a world that had nothing—nothing at all—to do with Black pain.

I have been wanting to explore the balance of reclamation and respite, to try and understand to what extent we've been held back from being whole, held and healed. About the varying needs for sanctuary, community, tradition and expression. I want every one of us, with this one beautiful life we are given, to be granted the access to live as many different lives as possible. To travel as much as we can—around the world, inside ourselves and with each other.

One of my favorite songs is "Zoom" by the Commodores. In it, the sky feels light and airy, life feels abundant with any and every possibility. The narrator, lead vocalist Lionel Richie, shyly sings about being a dreamer who believes that happiness exists somewhere, elsewhere, not here. The dreamer dreams of a place "where my mind can be fresh and clear" and believes that it is there that he'll "find the love that I long to see." I played this song almost every day of 2020 and 2021, on walks, on drives, as I showered. I let myself be a dreamer, fully disembodied from the world we live in right now, culturally cosmic. I gave myself up to bigger ideas and beliefs. I truly do believe that Black people create and express because we want to articulate and iterate the bounds of a better world than the one handed to us. I believe we know that this world exists and that we exist in it.

"Zoom" was composed by Ronald LaPread, the Commodores' lead guitarist. He conceived of the song while his wife, Kathy, steadily, mysteriously became ill due to stomach pains. He started the song one morning "fiddling around" on the piano and it was Kathy who came and sat next to him and said that while the song was nice the melody needed to "go up at a certain place." What they'd started wasn't initially finished, though, between LaPread's touring with the Commodores and Kathy's fast decline. Within months of being diagnosed with stomach tumors, she died at twenty-three.

But "Zoom" was finished by Richie, who'd been working on an incomplete song himself. In mourning, LePread left Richie to finish assembling the song and take the lead vocals. In a recount of the first recording of "Zoom," LePread said that after the song played, "everyone was crying."

I mention this because this tiny seven-minute song is an example of not only what we endure but what we can create together. It is a song that speaks to the power of love, the need for grieving, the strength in community and the profound importance of imagination. "Zoom" is an almost fifty-year-old song with a beautiful backstory and melody, which together illustrate the intersection of dreaming and creating. It is the prototype of getting to a certain higher place that Kathy talked about, a place, as Richie sings, "where everybody can be what they wanna be."

ACKNOWLEDGMENTS

This book was a culmination of love, community, friendship, collaboration and fun. I want to thank the early believers in me, my writing and *Black Genuis*: my mother Wanda Murphy-Price; my cousin Sean E. Vereen; my BFF Kendra Lee; my agent Sabrina Taitz (WME); and my rockstar attorney Sekou Campbell (Pierson Ferdinand). Shoutout to the first editor, Amber Oliver (formerly at Tiny Reparations), and then Lashanda Anakwah, who was the astounding editor who brought this book over the finish line.

Big love to the Penguin Random House/Dutton marketing and PR team, which included Diamond Bridges and Lauren Morrow.

So much love and support through the journey came from the aforementioned, but also Camilla Lee, Cheyenne Batista, Crystal Oliver, Devonayre Gooden, Dr. Erin Hadley, Gabriel Bryant, Idrissa Simmonds Nastili, Imran Siddiqquee, Maori Holmes, Miki Poy, Nicole Young, R. Eric Thomas, Sahara Clement, Zainab Ali.

ACKNOWLEDGMENTS

To the folks who were in my ear early on telling me, supporting me, and giving me opportunities to write—Aaron Beck, Brian Howard, David Fear, Jacob Brogan, Maryam Pugh, Myles Johnson, Natasha Alford, Scott Harrison.

To the writing pillars I love, laud and long to be like one day—Kiese Laymon, Deesha Philyaw, Doreen St. Félix, Kierna Mayo, my fellow writers in the Jack Jones "Culture, Too" Fellowship cohort.

To the people who opened their homes to me as I worked on this: Elana Aguilar and Stacey Goodman; Lee and Jeff Franklin; Gogo Ferguson; Tamara Weiss; Julie Taymor; Salem Mekuria; Michelle Molitor and Caroline Hill; Amy Schumer.

To all the cheerleaders who went sore in the throat—Akeem Anderson; Akeem Dixon; Alan Johnson, Atnre Alleyne and Tatiana Poladko; Beth Hagovsky; Bernadette Doykos; Damon Lindelof; Deborah Vereen; Ernest Price; Jennifer Wakefield; Kriste Dragon; Leona Christy and Catalyst:Ed; Iffy and Aaron Walker; Meladee Evans and Matt Munn; Nicole Jarbo; Rhonda Broussard; Saamra Mekuria-Grillo; Sharif El Mekki; Octavia & The 6.

To the outlets who put me on and gave me fertile thinking ground to draw inspiration for this book—PhillyMag.com, *Rolling Stone*, *TheGrio*, *Philadelphia Printworks*, *Vox*, *The Washington Post*, *Slate*.

To the institutions and organizations of inspiration, collabo-

ACKNOWLEDGMENTS

ration, and communication—BlackStar Film Festival, Amistad Research Center, HeinOnline.

And lastly to the departed along the way—Khadeejah Irvin, Miles Wilson, Jamil Gaines, Walter Aikens, Turner Cooper.

And my Dad, Z. Wayne Johnson, a mad Black genius of his own.

ABOUT THE AUTHOR

Tre Johnson was born in Trenton, New Jersey, and now finds himself in Philadelphia, where he writes with a focus on race, culture and politics. His work has appeared in *The Washington Post*, *Rolling Stone*, *Vox*, *The New York Times*, *Slate*, *Vanity Fair*, *TheGrio* and other outlets. He has provided media commentary on *CNN Tonight with Don Lemon*, *CBS This Morning*, *PBS News-Hour*, NPR's *Morning Edition* and other programs. In addition to writing, Tre is a career educator, working both inside and outside the classroom as a teacher and leader.

01 14